LIVING
in the
LIGHT

ALSO BY THE AUTHOR

Books

Awakening: A Daily Guide to Conscious Living

Creating True Prosperity

Creative Visualization

Creative Visualization Workbook

Developing Intuition

The Four Levels of Healing

Meditations

The Path of Transformation

Reflections in the Light: Daily Thoughts and Affirmations

Audios

Creative Visualization

Creative Visualization Meditations

Developing Intuition

Meditations with Shakti Gawain

Card Decks

Creative Visualization

Developing Intuition

25TH ANNIVERSARY EDITION

LIVING
in the
LIGHT

Follow Your Inner Guidance to Create a New Life and a New World

SHAKTI GAWAIN

with LAUREL KING

Nataraj Publishing

a division of

New World Library
Novato, California

Nataraj Publishing
a division of

New World Library
14 Pamaron Way
Novato, CA 94949

Copyright © 1986, 2011 by Shakti Gawain and Laurel King

Text design by Tona Pearce Myers

Library of Congress Cataloging-in-Publication Data
Gawain, Shakti, date.
Living in the light : follow your inner guidance to create a new life and a new world / Shakti Gawain, with Laurel King. — 25th anniversary ed.
   p. cm.
Rev. ed. of: Living in the light : a guide to personal and planetary transformation. c1998.
Includes bibliographical references.
ISBN 978-1-60868-048-1 (pbk. : alk. paper)
1. Self-actualization (Psychology) 2. Meditation. I. King, Laurel. II. Title.
BF637.S4G392 2011
158.1—dc23   2011036302

Originally published in 1986 by Whatever Publishing, now doing business as New World Library
First printing of 25th anniversary revised edition, December 2011
ISBN 978-1-60868-048-1
Printed in Canada on 100% postconsumer-waste recycled paper

New World Library is a proud member of the Green Press Initiative.

10 9 8 7 6 5 4 3

This book is dedicated

to the wisdom within us all.

Contents

Preface

Dear Friends,

I am thrilled to be releasing the 25th anniversary edition of my book *Living in the Light*. I am also grateful for the opportunity to still be teaching and writing after all these years. I never set out to be an author or leader in any intentional way. The process of personal development fascinated me and I was reading books and attending workshops on metaphysics, psychology, and Eastern philosophy. I soon found myself leading workshops sharing the ideas and practices that were helping me. I thought sharing them with others might be helpful. I didn't even start with the idea of writing a book! I was actually just looking for a way to organize these ideas and experiences and thought I could offer a pamphlet to people who were interested. Twelve books later(!), my work has evolved beyond my wildest dreams, in a way I could never have planned. I am so appreciative of all the support I have received over these years.

To date, my books have been translated into over thirty-five languages and have sold over ten million copies. In the publishing world, this is certainly considered a successful career. More important to me, however, it means that the information I have found so powerful and helpful in my own life is being shared with millions of people all over the world. My vision is that my work is helping people to make changes in their lives that broaden their experience and deepen their connection with themselves and others. I am touched by the messages I receive daily through mail, email, Facebook, and Twitter from people who have been touched by my work and found my books helpful.

This book made a powerful impact when it was first released. With the global shifts taking place now, this book is more timely and relevant than ever, and doing our own inner work is more critical. I see this anniversary edition as an opportunity to remind original readers of what is possible and to connect with new readers in empowering them to ignite their path.

Over the years since I wrote the first edition, my understanding has developed and (hopefully) deepened through my own life experience and my work with others. I felt that there were many things I would say somewhat differently now, and that perhaps it would be valuable to my readers to hear more of my ongoing story as well as some of my "older and wiser" perspective.

CREATIVE VISUALIZATION

One of the earliest workshops I attended was a course on developing healing power through intuition. At that time, I was still rather skeptical about this sort of thing and probably would never have gone to it except that my mother had taken the course and highly recommended it to me. I will never forget her description of a technique in which you can imagine what you want to have happen and it will very often come about. My mind felt doubtful about this but my heart made a leap and I remember thinking, "Ever since I was a child, I have always known that there is magic — that somehow, somewhere, magic really exists. This sounds like the closest thing to it that I have ever heard of."

I took the course and I was amazed! We started slowly and easily with simple techniques that anyone could accept and do, and gradually we worked our way into more unexplainable, but very powerful, processes. After five days, I had a strong psychic experience in which, for a period of several hours, I was able to consistently pick up specific information that I had no way of knowing except through my intuition. That experience began to dissolve some of the former limits on what I thought was possible.

One of the most important techniques I learned in that course was the basic technique of creative visualization — relaxing deeply and then imagining a desired goal in your mind exactly the way you want it to be. I started to practice this technique and found that it was amazingly effective. Quite often the things I imagined came true quickly and in unexpected ways. I became fascinated with the possibilities and took some other classes and workshops on similar subjects. I began to use creative visualization techniques in my life regularly and to teach them to my friends. Soon I began to lead workshops and do private counseling, and eventually I wrote *Creative Visualization.*

LISTENING TO INNER GUIDANCE

When I first discovered the techniques of creative visualization and found that they worked, I was excited because I felt that through using them I could create whatever I truly wanted in my life. This was an important step for me as it took me out of the essentially powerless attitude that I had had previously — the attitude that life is something that happens to you and that all you can do is make the best of it. It was in some ways a passive position — giving power to people and things outside of myself. Using creative visualization, I began to realize that much of the power rested in me, that to a great extent, I could choose to create my life the way I wanted it to be. It was very empowering and very freeing.

As I explored the process of creating my own reality, I gradually began to realize that the creative power I was feeling was coming from a source other than just my personality. For one thing, some of the things I *thought* I wanted didn't manifest; and, in retrospect, I could see that it was for my highest good that they didn't happen. Other things occurred so miraculously that it was as if some unseen force was putting everything into place. Sometimes I would have flashes of insight and awareness, or future visions, which were highly accurate and seemed to come from a source deep within myself. I became more and more interested in discovering what this creative force was all about and how it worked. I began to realize that "it" (my soul, or higher self) seemed to know more than "I" (my personality self) did about a lot of things. I saw that it would probably be smart to try to find out what that inner guidance was telling me, and follow it. Every time I did that, it seemed to work.

Eventually, I lost interest in trying to control my life, to make things happen in a way that I thought I wanted them to happen. I began to practice surrendering to the higher power of the universe within me and finding out what "it" wanted me to do. I discovered that, in the long run, it really wasn't that different. The universe seems to want me to have everything I truly want, and it seems to know how to guide me in creating it more effectively than I would know how to create it myself. The emphasis is different, though. Instead of figuring out what I wanted, setting goals, and trying to control what happened to me, I began to practice tuning in receptively to my intuition and acting on what it told me without always understanding why I was doing what I was doing. It was a feeling of letting go of control, surrendering, and allowing the higher power to be in charge.

The primary focus of my work now is on becoming conscious of the many different aspects of who we are, and learning to develop and express the infinite energies within us. This involves a great deal of what is often called "shadow" work — becoming aware of the parts of ourselves that we have denied or repressed because we feel they are unacceptable, and learning to value them and make them part of our lives. This healing work brings us into a greater and greater sense of balance and wholeness.

I understand, better than ever now, that "living in the light" involves traveling into the darker places within ourselves and shining the light of our consciousness into them so that we can truly love and express all that we are.

On this amazing human journey of ours, the strongest guiding force we have is right within us. We gain access to it through our intuitive sense, our "gut feelings" about what is right and true for us. The development of our relationship with our inner guidance is what this book is all about. May it serve you well.

With love,

Shakti Gawain

Part One

THE PRINCIPLES

Chapter One

A NEW WAY OF LIFE

*W*e are living in a very exciting and powerful time. On the deepest level of consciousness, a radical transformation is taking place. As the evolution of human consciousness gains greater and greater momentum, we are being challenged, on a planetary level, to let go of our present way of life and create a new one. In a sense, an "old world" is dying, and a "new world" is coming into being.

For many of us, simply described, the old world was based on an external focus — having lost our fundamental spiritual connection, we have believed that the material world is the only reality. Thus, feeling essentially lost, empty, and alone, we have continually attempted to find happiness and fulfill-ment through external "things" — money, material posses-sions, relationships, work, fame, food, drugs, and so on.

The new world is being built as we open to the higher power of the universe within us and consciously allow that creative energy to move through us. As each of us connects with our inner spiritual awareness, we learn that the creative power of the universe is inside of us. We also learn that we can create our own experience of reality and take responsibility for doing so. The change begins within each individual, but as more and more individuals are transformed, the mass con-sciousness is increasingly affected.

My observation that a profound transformation of con-sciousness is taking place in our world at this time is based on the changes I see within myself, in those around me, and in our society. It is affirmed by feedback I receive from thou-sands of people I work with all over the world.

Living in the Light is about this transformation of con-sciousness, within each individual and in the world. My use of the terms *old world* and *new world* throughout the book refers to the old way of living that we are relinquishing and the new one that we are creating.

For many people, this time may be distressing, because the world situation and/or our personal lives may seem to be going from bad to worse. It's as if many things are falling apart and will continue to do so with even greater intensity, but on the deepest level, I do not feel this is negative. It is upsetting to us to the degree that we are emotionally attached to our old way of living and steadfastly follow old patterns, rather than trying to open our eyes to the profound changes that are occurring.

Paradoxical as it may seem, these changes are the greatest blessing that any of us could possibly imagine. The truth is that the way of life that we have been following for centuries no longer works. While appropriate for its time, it cannot take us where we need and desire to go. The focus on materialism and the external world was necessary in a time when our primary challenge was physical survival. Our patriarchal values and the traditional roles of men and women may have been necessary in order to ensure the protection of our families for a certain period of time in our evolutionary process.

At this time, many human beings (and other species as well) on the earth are still struggling for physical survival. Yet there are an increasing number of us who no longer have to be preoccupied primarily with sheer survival. We have the opportunity, and thus the responsibility, to begin looking for deeper fulfillment on spiritual, mental, and emotional levels. We are searching for greater meaning and purpose in our lives, and for ways to live more responsibly and harmoniously on our planet.

While some people throughout history have led relatively meaningful and satisfying lives, I'm afraid that most of us have never found the fulfillment that we have yearned for. Our cultural conditioning has not given us the tools to develop a healthy connection with our inner realms of soul, intuition, and feeling, and to integrate them with our external world.

In a way, it's as if we've been in school for our entire lives, receiving an education that teaches the exact opposite of the way the universe actually functions. We try to make things work as we've been taught, and we may even enjoy some degree of success, but for most of us things never seem to work out as well as we had hoped. That perfect relationship never materializes, or if it does, it soon sours or fades away. Or it may seem as though there is never quite enough money; we never feel truly secure or abundant. Perhaps we don't get the appreciation, recognition, or success that we want. Even if we do achieve some of these things, we still may suffer from a vague sense that there must be something more, some deeper meaning. Some of us may actually connect with that deeper meaning and feel increasingly fulfilled and expanded by a growing spiritual awareness. Nevertheless, there are stubborn and sometimes puzzling old patterns and areas of life in which we experience great pain and confusion.

Thus, our first task in building the new world is to admit that our "life education" has not necessarily taught us a satisfying way to live. We must learn a way of life that is very different from the way we approached things before. This may not be easy for us, and it will take time, commitment, and courage. Therefore, it's very important to be compassionate with ourselves, to continually remind ourselves what a tremendous task we are undertaking. It will not be accomplished overnight; in fact, it is a lifelong process.

Just as a baby learns to walk by falling down repeatedly, we must remember that we are babies in the new world. We will learn by making lots of mistakes and often we may feel ignorant, frightened, or unsure of ourselves. But we would not get angry at a baby every time he fell down (if we did, he'd probably never learn to walk with full confidence and power), so we must try not to criticize ourselves if we are not able to live and express ourselves as fully as we wish immediately.

We are now learning to live more fully in accordance with the laws of the universe. We are challenged to explore all aspects of our human experience and to develop all levels of our being — the spiritual, mental, and emotional as well as the physical.

As we do this work, we experience an increasing sense of wholeness, empowerment, and aliveness, and a feeling of being "on purpose" in our lives. So, although letting go of the old world may seem difficult at times, it is well worth the commitment and hard work it takes to gradually make this transition into the new world.

Meditation

Sit or lie down, relax, close your eyes, and take a few deep breaths. As you exhale, imagine that you are letting go of everything that you don't want or need. Easily, without effort, let any frustrations, tiredness, or worries melt away. This is a time to release an old way of life that no longer works for you. Imagine that your old ways, your old patterns, and all the obstacles to achieving what you truly want are gently dissolved and leaving your body with each breath. Every time you exhale, and release a little of your old limitations, you create more space inside of you for something new.

After doing this for a few minutes, begin to imagine that every time you inhale you are breathing in life energy, the life force of the universe. Within this life energy is everything you need and desire — love, power, health, beauty, strength, abundance. Breathe it in with each inhalation. Imagine a new way of life opening up, filling you with aliveness, vitality, and energy. Pretend your life is exactly the way you want it to be. Imagine this new life is here, now, and savor it.

When the meditation feels complete, gently open your eyes and come back into the room. See if you can retain that sense of newness in yourself. Remember that you are now in the process of creating a new life for yourself.

Chapter Two

THE HIGHER POWER WITHIN US

*T*he foundation for life in the new world is built on the understanding that there is a higher intelligence, a fundamental creative power or energy in the universe that is the source and substance of all existence. The words and concepts that have been used to describe this power are innumerable. Here are just a few:

God	Spirit	Inner Guidance
Goddess	Essence	Higher Self
Higher Power	Being	The Universe
Source	Soul	Life Force
The Tao	The Force	Cosmic Intelligence

| Buddha Nature | The Light | Christ Consciousness |
| Great Spirit | I Am | All That Is |

These terms are attempts to express an experience or knowingness that is difficult to convey in words and rational concepts. Each of us has this experience within us; the words we choose to describe it are merely the labels that suit us best.

I seldom use the word *God*, as it has so many confusing connotations for so many. Frequently, people associate it with early religious training, which is no longer meaningful to them. I prefer terms such as *higher power, the universe, spirit,* and *inner guidance*. In this book, I will use some of these terms interchangeably to refer to our spiritual source, the essential creative intelligence and power within us. If any of these terms are not particularly meaningful to you, please feel free to substitute whatever word you prefer.

For the first twenty years of my life, my connection to the spiritual aspect of my being was largely undeveloped. I had no conscious experience of, or belief in, a higher power of any sort. I have had to move through many levels of doubt, skepticism, disbelief, and fear in order to arrive at the great trust I now have in the higher power of the universe that is within me and within everyone and everything that exists. I have not accepted anything on blind faith, so in a sense I have had to "prove" everything to myself through my life experiences. As I've learned to place my trust in the higher power of the universe and to live in accordance with universal principles, the changes I have felt and seen in my life have been truly miraculous.

Those of you who have felt deep spiritual awareness throughout your lives already have a solid foundation to build upon. For those of you who have felt spiritually "discon-nected," as I have, I hope my words will support and encour-age you to find this inner connection for yourself. There is no specific way to do this; everyone's experience is different. If this is something that you desire, ask within yourself that you be guided into an experience of your own spiritual nature. This may take some time, but if you desire it, it will happen. The words and exercises in this book may help you with this.

The universe has both personal and impersonal aspects; as I surrender and trust more, I find my relationship with this higher power becoming more personal. I can sometimes sense a presence within me, guiding me, loving me, teaching me, encouraging me. In this personal aspect, the universe can be teacher, guide, friend, mother, father, lover, creative genius, or fairy godmother. In other words, many of my needs and desires can be fulfilled through this inner connection. I often find the most powerful communion with the universe when I am alone, especially out in nature. At such times, the places inside of me that sometimes feel empty are filled with the energy of spirit. Here I find a guiding presence that nudges me in the direction I need to go and helps me to learn the lesson that lies in taking each step along my path.

Meditation

Sit or lie down in a comfortable position. Close your eyes and take a few deep breaths. Each time you exhale, relax your body more and more. Then take a few more deep breaths and, each time you exhale, relax your mind. Let your thoughts drift by without holding on to any of them. Allow your mind to go out of focus. Relax your awareness into a deep place within you.

Imagine that there is a very powerful presence within you. This presence is totally loving, strong, and wise. It is nurturing, protecting, guiding, and caring for you. At times it can be very strong and forceful. It can also be very light, joyful, and playful. As you get to know and trust it, it will make your life exciting, meaningful, and fulfilling.

You may get an image or a feeling or a physical sensation that represents this higher presence. Even if you don't see or feel a thing, assume it is there regardless.

Relax and enjoy the feeling or thought that you are being totally taken care of by the universe. Say this affirmation to yourself silently or aloud: "I feel and trust the presence of the universe in my life."

Chapter Three

INTUITION

Once we acknowledge the higher power of the universe, the obvious question arises: "How can we contact this power and gain access to it? How can we have an effective relationship with it?" After all, if there is within us a superior wisdom or a deeper knowledge than we normally experience, by tapping into it, we should be able to receive valuable guidance in how to live well in this confusing world. This realization began to dawn on me many years ago as I undertook my journey of consciousness. I have since discovered that the knowingness that resides in each of us can be accessed through what we usually call our intuition. By learning to contact, listen to, and act on our intuition, we can directly connect to this inner wisdom and allow it to become our guiding force.

This is where we find ourselves in opposition to life as most of us have been taught to live it in the old world. In modern Western civilization, we have learned to respect and even worship the rational, logical aspect of our being, and to dismiss, depreciate, or deny our intuition. We do acknowledge the ability of animals to seemingly understand things that are way beyond their rational capacity; we call this instinct. But it's a mystery that defies *logical* explanation, so we shrug our shoulders and dismiss it as something vastly inferior to the magnificent human ability to reason.

Our culture's entire value system is firmly based on the belief that the rational principle is superior and, in fact, constitutes the highest truth. The Western scientific tradition has become our religion. We are taught from a young age to try to be reasonable, logical, and consistent, to avoid emotional, irrational behavior, and to suppress our feelings. At best, feelings and emotions are considered foolish, weak, and bothersome. At worst, we fear they may threaten the very fabric of civilized society.

Our established religious institutions often support this fear of the intuitive, nonrational self. Once based on a deep awareness of the universal spiritual principle in every being, many religions only pay lip service to that idea now. Instead, they seek to control the behavior of their devotees, using elaborate rule structures purported to save people from their deep, irrational, and basically "sinful" natures. And according to many psychological disciplines, the dark and dangerous instinctual nature of man must be controlled. From this perspective, it is only the rational part of us that is capable of harnessing this mysterious force and channeling it into healthy, constructive modes.

In our worship of the rational and fear of the nonrational, we deny not only our emotions and our instinctual energies, such as sexuality and aggression, but also our natural intuitive sense, which is meant to be a primary guiding force in our lives.

Generally, less technically developed societies approach life with a deep awareness of, and respect for, the intuitive element of existence. Every moment of their daily lives is guided by a strong sense of connection with the creative force. However, it is their very lack of technical development that has contributed to their gradual destruction or subversion by modern civilization. Two examples we can look at are the Native American and African cultures. Both of these groups were devastated by their contact with European/American culture. However, a deep curiosity, respect, and appreciation for Native Americans has begun to surface in our awareness in recent times. And the African culture, forcibly brought to this continent, has probably done more than any other culture to keep the intuitive power alive in our country through its strong and soulful connection to spirit.

In human evolution, it seems that as our rational capacity has evolved, we've grown increasingly fearful of the other aspects of our nature. We've attempted to control these "dark forces" by creating authoritative rule structures that define right and wrong, good and bad, and appropriate and inappropriate behavior in a very heavy-handed way. We justify this rigid approach to life by blaming everything negative on nonrational nature — from our personal emotional dramas to social ills such as drug and alcohol addiction, crime, violence, and war.

The truth is that all aspects of our being are integral, important, and valuable parts of us. The more we distrust and suppress these energies, the more likely they are to eventually burst out in distorted ways. In other words, our problems are not necessarily caused by our emotional, nonrational nature running wild and uncontrolled; instead, both personal and social problems are more likely to be the result of fear and the suppression of our emotions, instinctual nature, and intuition. In this book, we are focusing on how we can reclaim the power of our intuitive sense.

Once we accept the reality of a higher power that is channeled to us through our intuition, it becomes clear that many of our personal problems and the ills of the world are actually caused by *not* following our intuition.

Our rational mind is like a computer — it processes the input it receives and calculates logical conclusions based on this information. The rational mind is finite; it can only compute the input it has received directly. In other words, our rational minds can only operate on the basis of the direct experience each of us has had in this lifetime.

The intuitive mind, on the other hand, seems to have access to an infinite supply of information. It appears to be able to tap into a deep storehouse of knowledge and wisdom — the universal mind. It is also able to sort out this information and supply us with exactly what we need, when we need it. Though the message may come through a bit at a time, if we learn to follow this supply of information piece by piece, the necessary course of action will be revealed. As we learn to rely on this guidance, life takes on a flowing, effortless quality. Our life, feelings, and actions interweave harmoniously with those of others around us.

It is as if each of us plays a unique instrument in a huge symphony orchestra, conducted by a universal intelligence. If we play our part without regard for the conductor's direction or the rest of the orchestra, we will have total chaos. If we try to take our cues from those around us, rather than the conductor, it will be impossible to achieve harmony — there are too many people, all playing different things. Our intellect is not able to process so much input and decide on the best note to play at each moment. However, if we watch the conductor and follow his direction we can experience the joy of playing our unique part, which can be heard and appreciated by everyone, and at the same time experience ourselves as part of a greater harmonious whole.

When we apply this analogy to our lives, we see that most of us have never realized a conductor is present. We have lived the best we can, using only our intellect to understand our lives, to figure out the best course of action. If we are honest with ourselves, we will readily admit that we are not making great music under the guidance of our rational mind alone. The dissonance and chaos in our lives and in the world certainly reflect the impossibility of living this way.

By tuning into the intuition and allowing it to become the guiding force in our lives, we allow our inner "conductor" to take its rightful place as the leader of the orchestra. Rather than losing our individual freedom, we receive the support we need to effectively express our individuality. Moreover, we will enjoy the experience of being part of a larger creative process.

I don't fully understand how the intuition functions in such an amazing way, but I definitely know, through direct experience and through observation and feedback from the many people I have worked with, that it does. And I find that the more I trust and follow this inner intuitive "voice," the easier, fuller, and more exciting my life becomes.

Meditation

Sit or lie down in a comfortable position in a quiet place. Close your eyes and relax. Take several slow, deep breaths, relaxing your body more with each breath. Relax your mind and let your thoughts drift, but don't hold on to any thought. Imagine that your mind becomes as quiet as a peaceful lake.

Now focus your conscious awareness into a deep place in your body, in the area of your stomach or solar plexus. It should be the place in your body where you feel that your "gut feelings" reside. This is the physical place where you can easily contact your intuition.

Imagine that you have a wise being living inside there. You might have an image of what this wise being looks like, or you might just sense that it is there. This wise being is really a part of you — your intuitive self. You can communicate with it by silently "talking" to it, making requests, or asking questions. Then relax, don't think too hard with your rational mind, and be open to receiving the answers. The answers are usually very simple, they relate

to the present moment (not the past or future), and they
feel right.

If you don't receive an immediate answer, let go and
go about your life. The answer will come later, whether
from inside of you in the form of a feeling or idea, or from
outside through a person, a book, an event, or whatever.

For example, you might say, "Intuition, tell me what I
need to know here. What do I need to do in this situation?"

Trust the feeling that you get and act on it. If it is
truly your intuition, you will find that it leads to a feeling of greater aliveness and power, and more opportunities
begin to open up for you. If it doesn't lead to these things,
you may have been acting not truly from your intuition but
from some other voice in you. Go back and ask for clarifi-
cation.

It takes practice to hear and trust your intuition. The
more you do it, the easier it will become. Eventually you
will be able to contact your intuition, ask yourself questions, and know that in that wise being within you, an
incredible source of power and strength is available to
answer your questions and guide you. As you grow more
sensitive to this guidance you will gain a sense of knowing
what you need to do in any situation. Your intuitive power
is always available to guide you whenever you need it. It
will open to you as you become willing to trust yourself
and your inner knowledge.

Chapter Four

BECOMING A CREATIVE CHANNEL

*T*o whatever degree you listen to and follow your intuition, you become a "creative channel" for the higher power of the universe. When you willingly follow where your creative energy leads, the higher power can come through you to manifest its creative work. When this happens, you will find yourself flowing with the energy, doing what you really want to do, and feeling the power of the universe moving through you to create or transform everything around you.

In using the words *creative channel*, I am *not* referring to the psychic process of trance channeling. Trance channeling involves a medium who goes into a trance state and allows another being to speak through him or her. When I use the term *channeling*, I mean being in touch with and bringing through the wisdom and creativity of *your own* deepest source. Being a channel is being fully and freely yourself and consciously knowing that you are a vehicle for the creativity of the universe.

Every creative genius has been a channel. Every masterwork has been created through the channeling process. Great works are not created by the personality alone. They arise from a deep inspiration on the universal level and are then expressed and brought into form through the individual personality.

A person may have great technical skill, but without the ability to connect with a deeper source, his work will be uninspiring. The difference between a technician and a channel was clearly demonstrated in the movie *Amadeus*. The composer Salieri knew how to write music but he didn't know how to tap into the creative source. Mozart wrote music that was both technically perfect and wonderfully inspired, and he did so easily, spontaneously, without thought or effort. From his early childhood on, music just seemed to bubble up and overflow from within him. I'm sure he had no idea how it happened and could not have explained to anyone else how to do it.

Such genius has always seemed mysterious and unexplainable, a God-given talent possessed by only a few. It seems to come and go at will — sometimes it's there, sometimes it's not. Because of this, many creative people fear their talent will suddenly disappear. They don't know how they got it so they have no idea how to recover it if it vanishes.

Creative people often function as channels in only one area of their lives (such as one of the arts, science, or business) and may have no idea how to do it in other areas of their lives. Thus, their lives can be terribly out of balance. (See the section "Highly Intuitive People" in the chapter "Trusting Intuition.") This is one reason that we often equate genius with emotional instability.

I believe we are all geniuses — each in our own unique way. We will discover the nature of our particular genius when we stop trying to conform to our own or other people's models, learn to be ourselves, and allow our natural channel to open. Through trusting and acting on our intuition, it's possible to bring our natural creative inspiration into every moment, into every area of our lives.

When I speak of a channel, I have an image of a long round pipe with energy flowing through it. It's somewhat like the pipe in a pipe organ, with the music coming through.

This channel image has three important features:

1. It is open and unobstructed inside so that the energy can move through freely.
2. It has a definite physical form; a structure surrounds the open space so that the energy is directed in a particular way. Without this structure, the energy would be free-floating, without any focus.
3. It has a power source — something that moves energy through the channel.

In a pipe organ, the power source (the organ) sends energy through the open pipes. The particular combination of open space inside each pipe and the structure — the size and shape of the pipe — causes a certain note to be sounded. The power source is the same for all the pipes and the energy moving through them is the same, but because each one is a different shape, each one makes a unique sound.

We can think of ourselves as channels similar to these pipes. We have a common power source (the universal life force), and the same creative energy flows through each of us. Our body and personality form the structure that determines the unique direction and function of each of us as a channel. It is up to us to keep our channel open and clear and to build and maintain a strong, healthy, beautiful body/personality structure as a vehicle for our creative energy. We can do this by constantly tuning in, asking where the energy wants to go, and moving with it.

A strong body/personality structure is not created by following anybody else's rules or good ideas about what you should eat, how you should exercise, or anything else. *It is created primarily by trusting your intuition and learning to follow its direction.* When deciding what to eat, how to exercise, or anything else, gather information from reliable sources, then check in with yourself to see what feels intuitively right for you, and do your best to follow your own inner guidance.

Most of us have had occasional experiences of trusting our intuition and having things work out in amazing ways. The following true story is a good example of this. My former editor, Becky, had achieved what many people think of as the "American dream." She had a husband and daughter, a good job, and money in the bank, and she owned her own home. Yet she felt an emptiness inside.

She felt an inner prompting to leave her job and pursue a

career in publishing. Her husband did not support this idea. In fact, he pointed out that she didn't have the "formal education necessary" to obtain a position in a publishing house.

Becky and her husband eventually separated, and she decided to make a move. She had been reading many books, including *Living in the Light*, and knew that she wanted to work for a publisher in the field of personal growth. Her intuitive feeling was that she needed to move to Northern California.

It was the most difficult and courageous step she had ever taken. She found herself in a new community with no friends, no job, and no money. She had no luck, at first, obtaining a publishing job, and so she looked for any kind of work that would enable her to survive. Many times she questioned her choice to take such a risk, yet she kept feeling a deep sense that she was on the right track.

Finally, she found work in another field. She was able to get back on her feet financially and she regained her confidence. She continued her search for a publishing job, and this time she was successful. She happily took a cut in pay and position to take an entry-level job at New World Library — the company she had always hoped to work for. Finally, she felt, she was at home. She ultimately landed her dream job as the editorial director.

By following her inner guidance, even through very difficult times, she found the perfect place to express her creativity and make her contribution to the world.

You may have had a similar experience, where listening to your intuition about something proved so fruitful and fulfilling. If so, the next step is to become more conscious of the process so you can recognize when you are following the flow of energy, as opposed to blocking, fighting, or trying to control it. The more willing you are to surrender to the energy within you, the more power can flow through you.

I know most of us have had experiences at certain times when we've felt life energy, wisdom, and power flow through us, when we have felt momentarily "enlightened." We have a brief moment of clarity and power and then it goes away again. When it goes away, we feel lost and unsure of ourselves.

The more you practice trusting and following your intuition, the more consistently you will feel that sense of "flow." At these times you may find yourself right where you want to be at every moment. You'll be where the energy is the greatest for you, doing what you want to do and watching miracles being accomplished. Your energy may have a transformational effect on others, as well.

As you strengthen the commitment to trusting yourself, everything in your life may change. At first, as you begin to let go of your old patterns, it may appear that things in your life are falling apart. You may find that you have to let go of certain things you've been attached to. Some relationships in your life may dissolve or simply "fizzle out" from lack of energy. Old pastimes may no longer interest you. You may even lose your job or decide to leave it.

Of course, these changes can be upsetting and frightening. Over time, however, you will find that this is all part of the transformation you are going through. As you learn to be true to yourself, you will find that you attract people, work, and other circumstances that reflect your evolution and development.

MAINTAINING YOUR FOCUS

In order to live fully and creatively, it's important to stay focused on following your own energy. This focus allows your channel to remain open to the energy flowing through. It's so easy to lose your focus, to get lost in other people, external goals, and desires. And the problem is, we do exactly that: we lose our connection with ourselves. As long as we are overly focused on the outside there will always be an empty, hungry, lost place inside that needs to be filled.

If I'm in love with someone and begin to think of him as my source of joy, then I lose myself. I have to remind myself that the source of joy and love is already within me, that I am experiencing love externally only because it is inside me. I try to keep the focus on the universe within and at the same time feel the universe coming through my lover to me.

For me, it's a constant discipline to remember to go back inside to connect with my intuition. I'll remind myself regularly during the day to do this. If I find myself getting lost in my outer activities, I'll check back inside to see if I'm being true to my feelings. This keeps the flow of the universe moving through me.

As we learn to pay attention to our intuitive feelings, follow our own energy and live our truth, we find that we feel more and more of the life force moving through us. That feeling of greater aliveness is so wonderful that it becomes our major focus and source of fulfillment.

We feel less attached to the externals of our lives. Whether or not things go as we have planned seems less important when we feel that our satisfaction is coming primarily from sustaining our connection to our own life energy. Ironically, when we stay true to ourselves in this way, the externals of our lives reflect our inner integrity. We attract to us and create around us exactly what our hearts and souls truly desire.

GOING WITH THE FLOW

Being a creative channel works in two ways: energy flows either through you to others or from others to you. For example, as I write my book, I focus on the energy flowing from the universe through me to others. Then, when people say to me, "I just love your books; they've changed my life," I am conscious of appreciation coming from them to me, and through me, back to the universal source.

As you become increasingly conscious of the flow of life moving through you and through everything and everyone else, your body will become capable of channeling more energy. The more energy you are willing to receive, the more you'll be able to give.

To become a clear channel for the universe presents the highest challenge and offers the greatest potential joy and fulfillment for every human being. Being a channel means living fully and passionately in the world, having deep relationships, playing, working, creating, enjoying money and material possessions, being yourself, yet maintaining your profound connection with the power of the universe within you, learning and growing from every experience that you have.

Then you can watch the universe create through you; it

can use you to do its work. Living as a channel is an ongoing learning process that's available to anyone who is willing to make the inner commitment.

THE POWER OF A GROUP

As we develop the ability to trust and follow our intuition, we learn to open and strengthen our individual channel so we can bring more power, creativity, and love through us. When we come together in a relationship or in a group, a group channel is created that is more powerful than any of us can be individually.

When many bodies and minds are willing to surrender, open up, and grow, these combined energies create a very strong, open structure that allows a lot more energy to come through from the universe. The process intensifies tremendously and everyone gets a powerful "boost" from the energy, which is capable of pushing each of us to the next level of our growth. Even though we may all be in somewhat different places and going through different things, each person receives the inspiration, the support, the push, or whatever is needed to enable him or her to take the next step of the journey. A group channel can open us up to a deeper level of awareness, and in the process, we share more of ourselves and find that we are healed of things that have held us back.

This is one reason I love teaching workshops and working with groups. My friends call me an "energy junkie" because I'm always attracted to situations in which the energy is most intense and expansive. I love the way my personal growth process is accelerated by the intensification that happens in groups.

I have found that in leading a group, I usually need to start with a certain amount of structure and take responsibility to clearly maintain the leader position. As the group continues, I can let go of the structure more and more and gradually allow the spontaneous energy of the group to take over.

As everyone surrenders and opens up, the group channel is formed. This process can be confusing and chaotic at times because, as the leader, I am no longer "in control" in the usual sense of the word. It can arouse my fears and everyone else's, but I find that when I'm willing to move through the fears, something powerful and beautiful emerges through the group channel. The universe leads us into new places and new discoveries that we would not have had an opportunity to experience if we had stayed within a more formal structure. I find the process of group channeling very exciting and rewarding.

In a sense, everyone living on this planet is a part of a gigantic group channel — the mass consciousness of humanity. This world, as it is now, is the creation of the group channel. As each one of us, individually, surrenders to the power of the universe and allows that power to transform and enlighten us, the group channel is affected accordingly. The mass consciousness becomes more and more evolved. This is how I see our world being transformed.

Meditation

Sit or lie down in a comfortable position. Close your eyes. Take a deep breath and relax your body. Take another deep breath and relax your mind. Continue to breathe slowly and deeply and let go of all tension or anxiety. As you relax, you find yourself in a deep, quiet place inside. Allow yourself to just rest in that place for a few moments, with nothing you need to do or think about.

From this deep, quiet place, begin to sense the life force within you. Imagine that you are following your own energy, feeling it, trusting it, moving with it in every moment of your life. You are being completely true to yourself, speaking and living your truth. You feel alive and empowered. Imagine that you are expressing your creativity fully and freely, and let yourself enjoy that experience. By being who you are and expressing yourself, you are having a healing and empowering effect on everyone you encounter and on the world around you.

Chapter Five

EXPLORING OUR MANY SELVES

*W*e are all born with an infinite number of different qualities, or energies, within us. One of our most important tasks in life is to discover and develop as many of these energies as possible, so that we can be well-rounded and experience the full range of our potential.

We can think of these energies as different archetypes, subpersonalities, or selves within us. In a way, it's as if there are many different characters living inside of us, each with its own task and purpose. Each of these selves has its own opinions, desires, even memories.

Since the physical world is a plane of duality, for each of these energies within us, there is an opposite energy. In order to experience wholeness and balance, we need to develop and integrate both sides of every polarity.

Most of us, however, are not accustomed to thinking in this way. We have been taught to think in a linear, exclusive fashion — good/bad, right/wrong. So if one quality is good or desirable, its opposite is bad, or undesirable.

For example, many of us have been taught that it is virtuous and admirable to give to others; a person who gives a lot is a good person. Therefore, the act of taking is thought to be selfish; a person who takes a lot for himself might be judged as less worthy than a giving person.

Someone with different values might think of this in an opposite way. He might admire a person who knows how to take a lot for himself and think of that person as smart and successful, while looking down on someone who is less aggressive and more giving as being foolish and easily taken advantage of.

Either way, one polarity is honored while the opposite is devalued. In reality, giving and receiving are equally important and valuable. If we give too much and aren't able to take or receive equally, we become depleted and resentful. If we take too much and are unable to give, we lose the satisfaction of making a contribution and incur the resentment of others. If we can give and receive more or less in balance, we experience a healthy sense of satisfaction.

From the time we are born, we begin to experiment with expressing the different energies within us. At that time we are completely dependent on our parents or caretakers for our survival and well-being, so we are extremely sensitive to their reactions to us. If we express an energy that invokes approval and positive attention, we are likely to continue to develop that quality. On the other hand, if something we do draws disapproval, criticism, or punishment, we are likely to discontinue it (unless that is the only form of attention we can get, in which case we may continue it).

Fairly soon, we have a pretty good sense of which energies help us get our needs met and which ones seem to cause us more problems than they are worth. This varies greatly according to each individual, family system, time period, and culture.

As we grow up, we continue to develop the energies that seem to work best to meet our needs. We become very identified with these qualities; that's who we think we are. These dominant energies become our *primary selves** — the inner characters whose job it is to take care of us and make our lives work as well as possible.

There is usually a group of primary selves who work together as a team, making most of our decisions for us. For example, some of my primary selves are the super-responsible one, the pleaser (who wants to make everyone happy so they will like me), the pusher (who wants me to work hard and accomplish a lot), the caretaking mother (who takes care of the child in other people so that they'll feel good with me), the consciousness teacher/healer. There are a number of others

---

* The ideas and terminology in this chapter, including the concepts of primary selves, disowned selves, and aware ego are derived from the work of Drs. Hal and Sidra Stone — the Psychology of Selves and the Voice Dialogue technique. For more information of their work, I highly recommend their books and tapes, listed in Recommended Resources.

on the team as well. They have all worked very hard to make me a worthy, well-loved, and successful person.

For every primary self, there is an opposite energy, which oftentimes has been repressed or denied because one way or another we got the message that it was not okay, or because it simply hasn't had space to develop. These energies become our disowned selves. They are usually buried within our psyche and we either don't know about them at all or are aware of them and try to hide them from the world. The *disowned selves* make up our shadow side, the parts of ourselves that we are embarrassed about, ashamed of, fearful of, or uncomfortable with. Our primary selves are usually working hard to make sure that we don't show these disowned selves to the world, since they are convinced that this would invite criticism, rejection, abandonment, or some form of disaster.

The problem is that each of these disowned selves carries an essential energy that is an important part of us. In fact, we are often in desperate need of these qualities in order to bring healing and balance into our lives. As long as we fear our shadow side, however, we can't access the energies that we need.

For example, if one of your primary selves is *power*, and you are very identified with being strong, competent, and independent, it is very likely that you have disowned your vulnerable side, the part of you that feels dependent on others and has needs for love and support. From the point of view of your power primary self, your vulnerable side might seem disgusting, and way too dangerous to show to the world for fear of being hurt. You might be completely unconscious of having a vulnerable side, or you might be aware of it but not want others to see it for fear of their judgment. Strangely, you will find that you are constantly attracting vulnerable people into your life, and you may at times feel very judgmental toward them for being so "weak."

The truth is that you need to become aware of, and accept, your vulnerable side. Without doing so, you are limited in your ability to experience true intimacy and closeness with others. Vulnerability is an essential piece of the human experience.

Life has an amazing way of confronting us with, and reflecting to us, the exact energies that we need to discover within ourselves and integrate into our lives. This happens through our dreams, where we are often shown symbolically the relationships between our primary selves and disowned selves. It happens constantly in our relationships, where others reflect to us the various different selves within us. Our imbalances show up in every area of our lives, from our health to our finances.

How do we become conscious of the many selves within and bring them into balance in our lives?

The first and most important step is to begin to recognize and become aware of our primary selves. What qualities and energies are you most identified with? Can you begin to notice the selves within you that automatically make most of your decisions and run your life?

We want to honor and appreciate our primary selves for how much they've done for us, while separating a bit from being totally identified with them. As soon as we become conscious of them as *energies within us* rather than *who we are*, we are beginning to develop what is called *aware ego*. Aware ego is the ability to recognize and hold all the different selves within us, so that we can have conscious choice about which ones we bring through at any given moment.

Once we have some awareness in relation to our primary selves, the disowned selves start to come forth. The primary selves usually remain our strongest qualities, but we begin to feel more balanced and our lives begin to work better as we begin to integrate the energy from previously disowned selves. The detachment from the primary selves, the development of aware ego, and the acknowledgment of the disowned selves is a gradual process that happens over a lifetime. Every step we take in this process, however, can make a big difference in our lives.

Our intuitive wisdom is one of the energies, or selves, within us. If we were encouraged to trust our intuition at an early age, or had an intuitive parent figure as an early role model, our intuition may be a primary self. Our culture tends to deny or minimize the intuitive function. For most of us, it is a disowned or relatively underdeveloped self. Conversely, many of us have developed a strong rational mind as one of the primary selves.

If rationality is a primary self, and intuition is disowned, in order to get in touch with our inner guidance, we may need to separate from over-identification with our rational side. We do this by recognizing it as *one aspect* of who we are, and beginning to notice how it operates in our lives. Once we become more aware of it in this way, we are no longer so identified with it and we can begin to have more conscious choice about how and when we use it. This creates space to explore our intuitive side as well.

If intuition is a primary self, and rational mind is disowned, we may have difficulty thinking logically or dealing with practical matters in a grounded way. In this case, we may need to develop our rational, practical side, in order to ground our intuition in the physical world.

OWNING OUR SHADOW SIDE

Every possible energy exists and needs to be acknowledged and accepted for us to find balance and wholeness in our lives. Any quality or energy that you are not allowing yourself to experience or express will come up inside and may be felt as conflict or a sense of "flip-flopping" or polarizing opinions within you. It will come up around you too, at work, at home, in your relationships, and will continue to trigger you or be an issue for you, until you recognize it as a part of you. Once you recognize it, you can begin to accept it and integrate it into your personality and your life.

Many people who are involved in personal growth become very identified with the energies and qualities that they think of as being "spiritual" — peaceful, loving, giving, and so on. In attempting to develop these aspects of themselves, they often deny and disown other aspects that they consider to be "unspiritual" — aggression, assertiveness, gut-level honesty, human vulnerability. Unfortunately, this simply creates a huge shadow side within them, which contributes to the collective shadow of denied energies in our world.

For some, it can be quite shocking to realize that if we over-identify with peace and love, and disown our inner warrior, we are not contributing to world peace. Quite the opposite, in fact. If we don't own our inner warrior and channel him in a constructive way in our lives, he retreats into the shadows of our individual and collective psyche, and actually contributes to the perpetuation of war on our planet.

If we are seeking inner peace, we must do the difficult and fascinating work of discovering and appreciating all aspects of who we are — truly making peace with ourselves. Consciousness is becoming aware of the many energies within us and accepting the essence of each quality. Exploring and embracing our darkness is the only way we can truly live in the light.

Meditation

Get into a comfortable position in a quiet place. Bring to mind one of your main personality characteristics or primary selves. Get a sense in your body of how that energy feels. Now imagine an opposite energy, which may be disowned or less developed in you. Imagine what that energy would feel like. What would be the positive benefits of developing more ability to contact that energy? How could that bring more balance into your life?

See if you can feel a balance of both of those energies at the same time. For example, if you are an outgoing person, you might balance that with a quieter, more introspective energy. If you are hardworking, you might balance that with the energy of relaxation or playfulness.

Chapter Six

OUR WORLD AS·OUR MIRROR

*T*he physical world is our creation: we each create our own version of the world, our particular reality, our unique life experience. Because I am creating my life, I can look at my creation to get feedback about myself. Just as an artist looks at his latest creation to see what works well and what doesn't, and thereby improves his skills, we can look at the ongoing masterwork of our lives to appreciate who we are and to recognize what we still need to learn.

We're creating our lives as we go along; therefore, our experiences give us an instant, ongoing reflection of ourselves. In fact, the external world is like a giant mirror that reflects our consciousness clearly and accurately. Once we have learned how to look into that mirror and perceive and interpret its reflection, we have a fabulous tool for self-awareness.

Understanding that the world is our mirror can help us see our lives as a reflection of our beliefs, attitudes, and emotional patterns. Viewed in this way, the external world can teach us about hidden aspects of ourselves that we can't see directly. The process is based on two premises:

1. I assume that *everything* in my life is my reflection, my creation; there are no accidents or events that are unrelated to me. If I see or feel something, if it has any impact on me, then I have attracted it or created it to show me something. If it didn't mirror some part of myself, I wouldn't even be able to see it. All the people in my life are reflections of the various characters and energies that live inside of me.

2. I always try to avoid putting myself down for the reflections I see. I know that nothing is truly negative. Everything is a gift that brings me to self-awareness — after all, I'm here to learn. If I was already perfect I wouldn't be here. Why should I get angry at myself when I see things I've been unconscious of? It would be like a first grader getting frustrated because she wasn't in college yet. I try to maintain a compassionate attitude toward myself and my learning process. To the extent that I can do this, the learning process becomes fun and really quite interesting.

When I view my life in this way, I can see it as a fascinating and adventurous movie. All the characters are parts of me played out on the big screen so that I can clearly see them. Once I see them and recognize their various feelings and voices inside myself, I can understand that they are all important and valuable parts of me that I need for my full expression in this life.

Continuing with this theme, if the movie portrays problems or struggles, I know I must check inside to find out where I might not be true to myself or have more learning and healing to do. I also know that when I'm trusting and being myself as fully as possible, everything in my life reflects this by falling into place easily and working smoothly.

PROBLEMS ARE MESSAGES

When there are problems in your life, the universe may be trying to get your attention. It's saying, "Hey, there's something you need to be aware of, something that needs to be changed over here!" If you pay attention to the small signals, you will learn from them. However, if you don't, the problems will intensify until you get the message and start to pay attention. If you accept that every time a problem occurs the universe is showing you something, you will make rapid progress on your journey of self-discovery.

When something "negative" happens, it's tempting to say, "Why does this happen to me? I'm doing the best I can but nothing seems to be going right. I can't understand why I keep having this problem." If you find yourself doing this, try to open up to another way of looking at things. Go within and say to the universe, "I know you're trying to show me something. Help me understand what it is."

After you do this, let go of focusing on it, and go about your life, but stay open to the message that will be coming through. It may come in the form of an inner feeling or awareness, some words from a friend, or something unexpected that happens to you. The message may come through immediately or it may take quite a while. One of my clients was fired, quite unexpectedly, over two years ago. At first, he was devastated, but after a few months of "getting his bearings," he went into business on his own. His business is now doing very well, but it was only a few weeks ago that he understood the message that his firing reflected. As he was talking to a friend about working for other people, he suddenly realized that the firing incident was trying to tell him that he was ready to be in business for himself, rather than working for other people. For him, this realization not only affirmed his present course in life but also finally resolved the sense of failure about being fired that had lingered with him since the incident.

INTERPRETING THE REFLECTION

The trickiest part of using the mirror process is learning how to interpret the reflection you see. Once you do get a message, but you're not quite sure what it is, how do you find out?

It will not help to over-analyze or obsess about it with your rational mind. It is far more effective to turn to your intuitive self, to ask the universe for help. Simply sit quietly, take a few deep breaths, and focus your awareness within — to the wise part of you that is in touch with the wisdom of the universe. Ask this part, either silently or out loud, for guidance or help in understanding the message. As you tune into your gut feelings and get a sense of what feels right in the moment, act on this feeling.

After acting on the feeling, try to be aware of the external and internal feedback from your actions. The external feedback is how well things work. Do things seem to fall into place and work easily? Then you're surely in tune with your inner guidance. If you're struggling to do something that doesn't happen easily, it's a message to let go and check back in to find out what you really want to be doing.

Internal feedback will come to you as feelings. If you feel empowered, more alive, then it's right. The ultimate key is *aliveness*. The more the universe moves through you, the more alive you feel. Conversely, every time you don't follow your inner guidance you feel a loss of energy, a loss of power, a sense of spiritual or emotional deadness.

In being true to yourself you will feel more alive, but you may also feel uncomfortable. This is because you are risking change! As you undergo certain changes, you may experience various intense emotions, such as fear, grief, or anger. Allow these emotions expression; after all, your inner guidance has to move through years of accumulated unconsciousness, denial, doubt, and fear. So let your feelings come up and wash through you — you are being cleaned out and healed.

At times like this, it is very important to have emotional support and a safe place to explore your feelings and do your healing process. If possible, I recommend finding a good therapist or support group — an environment where you are encouraged and supported in experiencing your own feelings and needs, expressing yourself honestly, and trusting your own sense of what's right for you. It's easy to be on a spiritual path where everything feels good and not want to deal with an emotional process that doesn't feel as good. However, by dipping into our emotional process, we ultimately have a richer experience of life.

When you are growing and changing rapidly, your inner doubts and fears will often be reflected in the reactions of those around you. If your friends and family question or judge the changes in you, recognize that they are simply mirroring the doubting, fearful voices in you, such as, "What if I'm doing the wrong thing? Can I really trust this process?"

Respond to such feedback from others in whatever way you feel is appropriate: reassure them, ignore them, argue with them, whatever. The important thing is to recognize that you are *really* dealing with your own inner fears. The conflicts you may experience with others are mirroring the conflicts within yourself, between the parts of you that want to grow and change, and those that feel safer to do things the way you've always done them. Affirm that you are learning to trust yourself more and more. You will be amazed to see how frequently others will begin to mirror your increasing self-trust and confidence by responding to you with trust and confidence.

Here are some examples of reflections:

If you experience feeling judged or criticized by others, you might be judging and criticizing yourself.

If someone is lying to you, there may be a way in which
   you are lying to yourself.
If you experience others being irresponsible in relation
   to you, you may be irresponsible in an area of your
   life.
If others are blaming you, you may be blaming yourself.
If you feel that others aren't listening to your feelings,
   you may not be listening to your own feelings.

Positive reflections are equally powerful:

If you love yourself, others will love you.
If you respect yourself, others will respect you.
If you trust yourself, others will trust you.
If you are honest with yourself, others will be honest
   with you.
If you are gentle and compassionate with yourself,
   others will treat you with compassion.
If you appreciate yourself, others will appreciate you.
If you honor yourself, others will honor you.
If you enjoy yourself, others will enjoy you.

CHANGING OLD PATTERNS

It's very important to realize that you may not be able to
change your old patterns overnight. Sometimes things seem
to change rapidly, once you've recognized the message, but
sometimes it seems like you keep doing the same thing and

getting the same unpleasant results long after you feel you know better. It takes time for the personality to change its habits, so you may have to watch the same old movie repeat itself a few more times.

If you feel your progress is too slow, ask the universe for help, and reach out for human help as well, by finding a therapist or support group. Change happens not by trying to *make* yourself change but by becoming conscious of what's *not* working. You can then ask your higher self for help in releasing the old and bringing in the new pattern. Remember, the darkest hour is just before the dawn — change often occurs just when you've given up, or when you least expect it.

USING THE MIRROR PROCESS

In using the world as your mirror, you must deal with the external realities of your life in whatever way you need to handle them. But as soon as possible, before, during, or after you deal with the externals, check inside to find out what is being shown to you.

For example, if someone is angry at you and blames or criticizes you, you may need to say to them, "Stop blaming me. I don't want to hear your judgments and criticisms of me. If you can talk about your own *feelings*, I'll be glad to listen, but if you keep attacking me, I'm going to leave." If they take more responsibility for their feelings (for example, "I felt hurt and angry when you didn't call me yesterday"), then you will probably be able to continue the conversation on a more productive level. If they continue to blame you and focus on your faults, you may need to support yourself by walking out of the room and refusing to continue the conversation until they stop their attack.

Either way, you have handled the *external* situation. Now, as soon as you get a chance, check inside yourself and ask, "I wonder what this person's anger is mirroring in me?" You may realize that you have been feeling very angry and critical toward yourself lately. Or perhaps you will discover that a part of you is upset because you have been focusing on others and not yourself. *When other people want more from you, it's usually an indication that you want more from yourself.* It may in fact be a signal that it's time to show up and be more present with your *own* needs and feelings. Interestingly, other people in our lives often start feeling better when we become more present with *ourselves*.

A friend of mine discovered that her boyfriend had been seeing another woman and lying to her about it. She was very hurt and angry, particularly to discover the dishonesty. They had a long talk in which she was able to express her feelings to him. Then she took some time alone for a while to sort things out on her own.

When she was alone, she asked herself, "Is there some way I'm lying to myself, some way I'm not being totally truthful and honest with myself?" She let go of thinking about it and went to work. By the end of the day she realized she had often felt this man was not fully present with her, was not being real with her. But in the past, she had denied and covered up these feelings because she was afraid to confront him with what she felt and intuitively knew. Thus, she effectively lied to herself and supported him in his deceptions as well.

She realized this was a lesson in learning to trust her feelings more and to have the courage to express and support them. She started to do this more with her boyfriend, and they eventually worked out a more honest, communicative relationship. She might also have chosen not to continue the relationship. What matters is that she received the gift from it — learning to trust and express her feelings.

If you are emotionally triggered by something a person does, the two of you are probably mirrors for each other. It may appear that you have opposing viewpoints, but internally you are probably similar. One of you is acting out one side of the internal conflict, while the other plays out the other side.

For example, one person may want more commitment in a relationship, while the other wants more freedom. They become extremely polarized on this issue and truly believe they want opposite things. However, if one person suddenly switches her position (the one who wanted commitment suddenly wants freedom), the other person often swings to the opposite polarity. The reason for this is that they are attempting to resolve an inner conflict they *both* have — the desire for closeness and security and the need for independence and autonomy (which may feel like the fear of loneliness versus the fear of entrapment).

Once people look inside and become more aware of their feelings, they often recognize that they have simply projected their inner conflict onto the outside world so that they could recognize and deal with it. If a person truly and unequivocally wants a committed relationship, he will simply attract another person who wants the same thing. If someone feels completely clear about wanting to explore being with many partners, he simply does it. By using the mirror process, you can recognize what you really feel and learn to be more honest with yourself. Once you recognize an internal conflict, you can acknowledge that both polarities are really within you and find ways to honor both of the energies. For example, we all contain the polarities of desiring closeness in relationships while also desiring independence and autonomy. As conscious beings, we must learn to satisfy *both* these needs. By honoring both of these energies within us, we can learn to create relationships in which we have both closeness and independence.

Seeing the world as your mirror also gives you wonderful opportunities to receive positive feedback. Think of everything that you like and enjoy about your life right now. You created these things — they are also your mirrors. Think of the people you know whom you love, enjoy, respect, and admire. They are your mirrors. They couldn't even be in your life if they didn't reflect you: you would not be able to recognize their positive qualities if you didn't have similar ones. Think of the people and animals that love you. They are a mirror of how you love yourself. If you have a home that you love, or a particular spot in nature that is very beautiful to you, it is a mirror of your own beauty. When you see beauty anywhere, it's a reflection of yourself.

There are mirrors everywhere. Whoever you have a connection with is a mirror for you, and the deeper the connection, the stronger the mirror. Part of the fascination in using the mirror process is discovering who we are through these external reflections. The key is to always go back inside to discover the meaning of the reflection for you. The more you are willing to do that without either rationalizing away what you see or blaming yourself for it, the faster you can develop and express the multifaceted potential within you.

Meditation

Relax and close your eyes. Take a few deep, slow breaths and move into a deep place inside of you. Bring to your mind an important person or thing in your life and ask him/her/it what it is mirroring to you. Stay open to receiving the answer, whether it comes in words, feelings, or images. It may come immediately or some time later.

Exercises

1. Think of a person you especially love and admire. List all his or her positive qualities. Think about how those qualities mirror you. In some cases, they may be qualities you have not fully developed in yourself. Recognize that this person is here to teach and inspire you by his or her example.

2. Make a list of the things and people in your life that you especially like. Praise and appreciate yourself for creating and attracting these mirrors.

3. Think of someone whom you judge or feel uncomfortable with. Try to figure out exactly what quality they have that you dislike. Is it possible that this is a quality within yourself that you deny or judge, and that your life could be enhanced if you made

peace with, and were able to express, that part of yourself?

For example: If you dislike someone who appears very selfish, that person may be reflecting the disowned part of you that wants you to pay more attention to taking care of your own needs. Perhaps you are overly identified with taking care of others.

Chapter Seven

SPIRIT AND FORM

Spirit is the essence of life, the energy of the universe that creates all things. Each one of us is a part of that spirit — a divine entity. So the spirit is the higher self, the eternal being that lives within us.

Form is the physical world. As an individual, my form is my physical body and my personality, which includes my mind and my emotions. It is also my self-concept — my ego/identity structure: "My name is Shakti Gawain. I was born on September 30, 1948. I'm 5'9" tall. I'm intelligent and have a generally outgoing personality." This is all information about my form.

We, as spiritual beings, created the physical world as a place to learn. It's our school, our playground, our artist's studio. I believe that we're here to master the process of creation and to learn how to integrate all levels of our being — spiritual, mental, emotional, and physical — so that we can live in the physical world in balance and wholeness.

Physicists are now discovering what metaphysicians have claimed for thousands of years: seemingly solid physical matter is, in reality, made of energy. If we look through a powerful microscope at anything "solid," we see an infinite number of little vibrating particles. If we closely examine one of these particles, we discover that it is made of even smaller particles, and so on. The fact is that everything physical is made of energy — which we can also call "life force," or "spirit." So modern science supports the ancient metaphysical truth that form is created out of spirit.

When our spirit decides to manifest as physical form, the first thing it creates is a physical body in which to house itself. We choose a life situation and create a body in accordance with what we feel will best serve and teach us in this lifetime. Ultimately, our goal is to create a body/personality that can fully express our divine creative spirit, a form that can do everything our spirit wants to do easily, skillfully, and beautifully.

However, our physical form (body/personality) has an important job of its own to do. Its main responsibility is to make sure that we survive physically, and once that is assured, that we actually *thrive* physically and emotionally in this life. So our forms have a certain consciousness that revolves around making sure we get enough food and shelter, protecting ourselves from danger, gaining a sense of security by making sure reproduction takes place and offspring survive, creating family and community in which we can give and receive the emotional nurturing we need, and finding a sense of belonging.

The energy of our spirit is very different from that of our form. Our spirit has a very expanded vision and perspective, but very little understanding of what it means to be in a human form. Our form carries our human experience, with all its limitations and vulnerabilities, and also with the knowledge of how to live in the physical world.

After we are born into the body, most of us forget who we are on the spiritual level and why we came here. We take on the "survival" consciousness of the physical world and we get lost in the world of form. We forget that we are souls, believing we are just our personalities. We lose touch with our source of power and feel lost and helpless. Life becomes a tremendous struggle to find meaning and satisfaction.

We may spend many lifetimes caught up in this cycle. Certainly, most of us have spent many years in this lifetime looking outside ourselves, trying to find fulfillment in the world of form. Eventually we realize that it's not working: no matter what we do in the world, we don't find profound happiness. We become unwilling to spend one more lifetime, one more year, or even one more minute in futile struggle. In frustration and hopelessness, we give up.

This is usually a painful and frightening time in a person's life — it feels like hitting bottom. It is a kind of death of our old identity when the form recognizes the hopelessness of trying to live this way and surrenders its fight. It would rather die than keep trying. At this time a person often has thoughts and feelings of death, or may experience the death of a close friend or family member (or several of them). Some people create a serious illness, accident, or other major crisis at this time, and some contemplate or even attempt suicide.

But the darkest hour is truly just before the dawn. When we finally give up the struggle to find fulfillment "out there," we have nowhere to go but within. It is at this moment of total surrender that a new light begins to dawn. When we give up our old way of doing things, we create space for a new energy to come through.

This is like being reborn. We are infants in this new world and have no idea how to live since none of our old ways work here. We feel uncertain and out of control. Yet hope is reborn in us, and a new power and vision start to come through. This can be the beginning of developing a form that is conscious of, and integrated with, our spirit.

Ram Dass has a beautiful analogy for this process. He likens it to a clock, where 12:00 is the starting point. From 12:00 to 3:00 life is totally lost in the world of form. From 3:00 to 6:00 is gradual "disillusionment" with the world, and 6:00 is when you hit bottom. You feel that you lose everything, but as you pass through 6:00 you are actually waking up to reconnecting with spirit. From 6:00 back up to 12:00 is ever-increasing integration of spirit and form. As individuals, we are at various stages in this process. I have a sense that we each have one major cycle of this type lasting over many physical lifetimes, and we also have an infinite number of minor cycles — sometimes almost daily!

When we, as individuals, first rediscover our spirit, we are usually drawn to nurture and cultivate this awareness. This often involves withdrawing from the world to one degree or another, and going within. For some people this takes the form of spending time in nature; for some it involves practicing meditation, going to retreats, and so forth; for some it may be simply finding time to be alone and quiet. Often it's a time of partial or complete withdrawal from relationships, work, and/ or other attachments that tend to pull us outside of ourselves. For some, this phase may last only a few weeks or months. Each of us is unique, so we all experience this shift within in different ways. In one way or another, we learn to go inside and be in that quieter place in ourselves for a while. There we find a deeper and deeper connection with our spirit.

While we are deeply connected with ourselves in this way, we often find that we have a feeling of clarity, vision, wisdom, power, and love. This is because in that moment, we are connected with the expansive energy of spirit, and not distracted by the problems and responsibilities of dealing with the world of form.

If we choose to follow one of the traditional spiritual paths we may remain more or less withdrawn from the world. In this way we can be true to our spirit and avoid dealing with the attachments and patterns of our form. Unfortunately, we never have the opportunity to fully integrate spirit and form.

In order to create the new world, we are being challenged to move out into the world of form with full spiritual awareness. We need to recognize the differences between our spirit and our form and learn to integrate them.

INTEGRATING SPIRIT AND FORM

The first step in the process of consciously integrating form and spirit is to be able to *recognize* and *feel* both the consciousness of your spirit and the consciousness of your form. You may be accustomed to feeling only one of them most of the time, with occasional flashes of the other. Or you may flip back and forth frequently between the two perspectives. It's as if one takes control of the body for a while and you see things from that viewpoint. Then the other one takes over and suddenly everything looks quite different.

This understanding can explain a lot of things that many of us are experiencing in our lives. Why is it that we have wonderful moments of consciousness and clarity, and then find we have completely lost our perspective and become immersed in fear and pain again? How is it that we can feel so loving, wise, and accepting one day and the next day feel so angry, foolish, and judgmental? Why did we feel as if we'd really "gotten it" at a workshop and then seem to "lose it" the next day? How is it that we can feel so peaceful and unattached when we are meditating, yet often our relationships seem like a worse mess than ever? And how come we have such trust in the abundance of the universe but we're still having financial problems?

The answer is simple — we are dealing with the discrepancies between spirit and form. This is a very difficult thing to confront, and we are facing a real challenge. Many people reach this point and have a hard time going any further.

For example, I frequently get inspiring, creative ideas for a new project I want to do. I get a very strong vision of how wonderful it will be and how it can work. All this is coming from my spirit, of course. I get very excited and jump into the project, making all kinds of plans and initiating many actions in that direction. A few days or weeks later I find myself feeling totally overwhelmed, overworked, frustrated, and ready to throw the whole thing out the window. My spirit had a true vision, but I was trying to achieve it without regard for the needs of my human form. At this point I have to stop and consider what's realistic for me, then set the project aside for a while, or allow it to take longer and develop more slowly. My spirit tends to race ahead, so it has to learn to go at the pace my form can handle.

The second step is to *love* and *accept* both aspects of yourself. They are both beautiful and vital parts of you. Without your spirit you wouldn't be alive — you'd only be a dead body! Without your form you wouldn't be able to be in this world — you'd be existing in some other realm of consciousness.

It may be frustrating at times to see that your form can't live up to all the ideals that your spirit may have. It's important to recognize that our form has its own wisdom and the spirit can learn from the form just as the reverse is true. After all, we chose to come to this plane of existence in order to experience being human!

For example, many years ago I was living with a man and we had an "open relationship" — in other words, we were free to be with other lovers. I had a strong spiritual ideal that I could love someone deeply and allow him to be free to follow energy he might feel with someone else, while I was free to do likewise. Sometimes I was able to do this, briefly, and I had some beautiful moments when I felt an expansive and exhilarating unconditional love. But most of the time I was overwhelmed with jealousy and emotional pain. I finally realized that my spiritual ideal simply did not fit the reality of my human feelings and needs. It became very clear to me that I could only experience the kind of emotional intimacy that I wanted in a monogamous relationship.

One important key to integrating spirit and form is learning to listen to your intuition and act on it. Your inner guidance will always move you in the direction of greater balance and integration between form and spirit. Even in the process of learning to trust your inner guidance, however, you can't move faster than your form is ready to go.

Here is a very important point: You cannot force your form to trust and follow intuition through *will*. You must allow it to educate itself through conscious observation.

In other words, you can't force yourself to always follow your intuitive feelings, even though you desire to live that way. Sometimes it may seem like too big a risk; even though your spirit knows it would work out, your form is too afraid to do it. Don't push yourself past what you are ready to do. Simply observe the process and be honest with yourself about how it feels and what happens. Then the change will happen naturally and spontaneously.

For example, suppose you are with a friend and there's something you want to say but you are afraid to do so for fear your friend will get hurt or angry and reject you. If you find you do have the courage, go ahead and say what you feel. Then observe what happens and how you feel as a result. Chances are good that you will feel energized and empowered by the experience.

If, on the other hand, you are too afraid to speak the truth, don't try to push yourself past your fear. Again, simply observe yourself being with your friend and not being totally yourself. Notice that you feel deadness and loss of energy; you may also feel resentful toward your friend. *Try not to judge yourself for your lack of action. Remember, this is a learning process.*

The spirit usually tends toward expansiveness, risk taking, and change. The form often tends toward what it perceives to be safety, security, and the status quo, because its basic task is to make sure we survive and it fears that change might mean disaster or death.

If you are able to observe yourself without rationalization or judgment, you will begin to notice that when you trust yourself and follow your energy fully, you feel better. Conversely, when you are controlled by old patterns of fear and holding back, you feel worse. After a while, your form gets the message clearly and begins to *spontaneously* follow the energy instead of the old pattern because it knows it will feel better. Eventually you have a form that automatically goes for the most alive energy in every situation, without having to think about it and control it.

In this process of learning to trust yourself, many old feelings and deep emotional patterns will come to the surface to be healed and released. This is a very important part of it, and must be allowed to happen. Old memories and experiences may be triggered. Feelings of sadness, fear, pain, guilt, and rage may come up. Allow yourself to feel all of them, allow them to wash through you; they will be released. They are being cleared out of your form. As the light of spirit penetrates every cell of your body, it dispels the darkness.

As you learn to consciously observe the transformation process, you will watch yourself repeating a lot of old patterns long after you seemingly know better. Spiritually and intellectually, you realize there is another way, but emotionally, you are still clinging to the old habits. This is a difficult time. Try to be patient and compassionate with yourself. When you recognize the futility of an old pattern so clearly, it's about to change! A short time later, you will suddenly begin to respond differently, in a more positive way.

As you do the work of integrating spirit and form you may see your physical body change and become lighter, stronger, more clearly defined, healthier, and more beautiful. Because your life is your creation and the mirror of your transformation, all the forms in your life — your work, money, car, house, relationships, community, the world — will increasingly express the power and beauty of your spirit.

Meditation

Get comfortable, relax, and close your eyes. Take a few deep breaths and relax your body and mind completely. Allow your conscious awareness to move into a deep, quiet place within you.

Imagine that there is a beautiful golden light radiating from a place deep within you. It begins to grow and expand until it fills your entire body. It's very powerful, and as it fills you, it penetrates into every cell of your

*body, literally waking up each molecule to the light. Imag-
ine your entire body glowing and radiating with this light.
Then see and feel your body being transformed — becoming healthier, stronger, and more beautiful. Imagine
everything else in your life being similarly transformed.*

Exercise

See if you can observe yourself nonjudgmentally and notice
when you are able to listen to your intuitive feelings and act on
them, and when you are not. Observe how you feel and what
happens in each of these situations. Ask your higher power to
help you learn to trust and follow your energy more and more.

Chapter Eight

THE MALE AND FEMALE WITHIN

*E*ach of us has male and female energies within us. I believe that one of the most important challenges we have in this world is to develop these energies fully, so they can interact in harmony with each other.

Eastern philosophies have always included the concept of yin (feminine/receptive) and yang (masculine/active) and have said that everything in the universe is made up of these two forces. In the West, Carl Jung did pioneering and exciting work with his concept of the anima and the animus. He explained that men have a feminine side (anima) and women have a masculine side (animus), that most of us have strongly repressed these aspects of ourselves, and that we must learn to come to terms with them. He and his followers have done wonderful work using dreams, myths, and symbols to help men and women reclaim the lost, denied parts of themselves. Many other philosophers, psychologists, poets, playwrights, and artists have expressed the ideas of masculine and feminine energies within ourselves and within everything.

Some people have resistance to the words *female* and *male*, because in our culture we have so many preconceived ideas about what those words mean, associate so much emotional "charge" with them. If it's more comfortable for you, substitute the words *yin* and *yang*, *active* and *receptive*, *dynamic* and *magnetic*, or any other words that appeal to you.

THE MASCULINE AND FEMININE

I think of our female aspect as our intuitive self. This is the deepest, wisest part of ourselves. This is the feminine energy, for men and women. It is the *receptive* aspect, the open door through which the higher intelligence of the universe can flow, the receiving end of the channel. Our female communicates to us through our intuition — those inner promptings, gut feelings, or images that come from a deep place within us. If we don't pay conscious attention to her in our waking life, she attempts to reach us through our dreams, our emotions, and our physical body. She is the source of higher wisdom within us, and if we learn to listen carefully to her, moment by moment, she will guide us perfectly.

The male aspect is action — our ability to do things in the physical world — to think, to speak, to move our bodies.

Again, whether you are a man or a woman, your masculine energy is your ability to act. It is the outflowing end of the channel. The feminine receives the universal creative energy and the masculine expresses it in the world through action — thus, we have the creative process.

Our female is inspired by a creative impulse and communicates it to us through a feeling, and our male acts on it by speaking, moving, or doing whatever is appropriate.

For example, an artist might awaken with an inspired idea for a painting (an image communicated from his female) and immediately go into his studio, pick up his brush, and begin painting (action taken by his male).

A mother might feel sudden concern for her child (a warning from her inner female), and run into the other room and pull the child away from a hot stove (action taken by her male).

A businessperson might have an impulse to contact a certain associate (guidance from his or her female), make a call (action taken by his or her male), and put together a new deal.

In each case, when the male and female within were in creative union, there was a creative result — a painting, saving the child, a business enterprise. Even the simple sequence of feeling hungry, going to the kitchen, and fixing a meal illustrates the same process.

The union of feminine and masculine energies within the individual is the basis of all creation. Our female intuition plus our male action equals creativity.

Having your female and male energies fully developed and integrated will allow you to live a harmonious and creative life. To fully integrate the inner male and female, you need to put the female in the guiding position. This is her natural function. She is your intuition, the door to your higher intelligence.

Remember now that I am talking about an *internal* process in each of us. Sometimes people externalize this idea and think I'm saying that men should let women tell them what to do! What I'm actually saying is that we *each* need to let our intuition guide us, and then be willing to follow that guidance directly and fearlessly.

The nature of the feminine is wisdom, love, and clear vision expressed through feeling and desire. The male nature is all-out risk-taking action in service to the feminine, much like the chivalrous knight and his lady.

Through his surrender to her and his action on her behalf, our male energy builds a personality structure within us that protects and honors the sensitive energy of our intuitive female. I often imagine my male as standing behind my female — supporting, protecting, and "backing her up." For a man, the image might be reversed — you might see your female as within or behind you, guiding, empowering, nurturing, and supporting you. When these two energies are thus in harmony and working together, it's an incredible feeling: a strong, open, creative channel, with power, wisdom, peace, and love flowing through.

AN IMAGE

Every now and then I do a visualization process in which I ask for an image of my male and female. Each time I do it, I receive something a little different that teaches me something new. I'm sharing with you one of the most powerful images, because it is such a dramatic illustration of one aspect of the relationship between inner female and male.

My female energy appeared as a beautiful, radiant queen, overflowing with love and light. She was being carried through the streets on a litter borne by several carriers. The people were lining the streets, waiting for an opportunity to see her. She was so beautiful, open, and loving that as she passed by, waving, smiling, and throwing kisses to people, they were instantly healed of any pain or limitation.

By her side walked a samurai warrior carrying a sword. This was my male energy. It was well understood by everyone that if anyone made a threatening move toward the queen, he would instantly raise his sword and ruthlessly cut down the offender. Knowing this, naturally, no one dared to harm her.

He was willing to be absolutely unhesitating in his trust of his own judgment and his own response, which left her completely safe and protected. Feeling totally safe, having no need to hide or defend herself, she was free to be completely open, soft, and loving and to give her gifts freely and generously to all around her.

Meditation

Sit or lie down in a comfortable position and close your eyes. Take a few deep breaths and relax your body and mind completely. Allow your conscious awareness to move into a quiet place within you.

Now bring to your mind an image that represents your inner female. This image could be an actual person, an animal, or something more abstract — an energy, a color or shape, or simply a feeling. Spontaneously take whatever comes to you.

Take a look at your female and get a sense or a feeling of what she represents to you. Notice some of the details of the image. Notice the colors and textures. Notice how you feel about her.

Ask her if she has anything she would like to say to you right now. Allow yourself to receive her communication, which may or may not be in words. You may also ask her any questions you have. There may be something you want to know from her. Again, receive her communication to you, whether it comes in words, a feeling, or an image.

Once you have allowed yourself to receive her communication, and you feel complete for this moment, take a deep breath and release her image from your mind. Come back to a quiet, still place.

Now draw to mind an image that represents your male self. Again, take what image comes to you. It could be an image of an actual man or it could be some abstract symbol or color. Explore this image. Begin to notice the details of it. Notice its colors and texture. Notice how you feel about it. Then, ask your male self if he has anything to communicate to you at this time. Be receptive to receiving his communication, whether it is in words or some other form. If you have anything you want to ask him, do this now. Be open to any words or images you may receive. If an answer doesn't come to you immediately, know that it will come later.

Once you feel complete with your communication with him, release his image from your mind. Come again to a quiet place inside.

Now ask for the images of both your male and female to come to you at the same time. See how they relate to each other. Are they in relationship to each other or are they separate? If they are in relationship to each other, how do they relate? Ask them if they have anything they would like to communicate to the other or to you. Stay open to what comes to you in words, images, or feelings. If you have anything you'd like to say to them or ask them, do that now.

When you feel complete, once again take a deep breath and release their images from your mind. Come back to a quiet, still place inside.

Exercise

Close your eyes and contact your female intuitive voice. Ask her what she wants — is there a gift she desires or something she wants to say or do? When she has told you what she wants, imagine your new male supporting her desire. See him taking any necessary action to honor her need and desire.

When you open your eyes, do your best to follow whatever you feel your intuition wants you to do.

Chapter Nine

MEN AND WOMEN

*W*e all instinctively understand the basic functions of feminine and masculine energies, but we may not realize that they both exist in each person. More often we tend to associate male and female energies with their respective body types.

Thus, women have become the symbols of female energy. Traditionally, women have developed and expressed receptivity, nurturing, intuition, sensitivity, and emotion. In the past, many women more or less repressed assertiveness, direct action, intellect, and the ability to function effectively and strongly in the world.

Likewise, men have become the symbols of male energy.

Traditionally, they have developed their ability to act in the world strongly, directly, assertively, and aggressively. Many men repressed and denied their intuition, emotional feelings, sensitivity, and nurturing.

As we cannot live in the world without the full range of masculine and feminine energies, each sex has been helplessly dependent on the other half for its very existence. From this perspective, each person is only half a person, dependent on his or her other half for survival. Men have desperately needed women to provide them with the nurturing, intuitive wisdom, and emotional support without which they unconsciously know they would die. Women have been dependent on men to take care of them and provide for them in the physical world, where they haven't known how to take care of themselves.

It might seem like a perfectly workable arrangement — men help women, women help men — except for one underlying problem: as an individual, if you don't feel whole, if you feel your survival depends on another person, you are constantly afraid of losing them. What if that person dies or goes away? Then you die, too, unless you can find another such person who is willing to take care of you. Of course, something might happen to that person also. Thus, life becomes a constant state of fear in which the other person is merely an object for you — your supply of love or protection. You must control that source at any cost: either directly, by force or superior strength, or indirectly using various manipulations. Generally, this happens subtly — "I'll give you what you need so you will be just as dependent on me as I am on you, so you will keep giving me what I need."

So our relationships have been based on dependency and

the need to control the other person. Inevitably, this leads to resentment and anger, most of which we repress because it would be too dangerous to express it and risk losing the other person. The repressing of all these feelings leads to dullness and deadness. This is one reason why so many relationships start off exciting ("Wow! I think I've found someone who can really fulfill my needs!") and end up either filled with anger or relatively dull and boring ("They aren't fulfilling my needs nearly as well as I had hoped, and I've lost my own identity in the process, but I'm afraid to let go for fear I'll die without this person.").

FINDING THE BALANCE

In recent times, of course, the strongly separated roles of men and women have begun to shift. In the past two generations, increasing numbers of women are exploring and expressing their abilities to act in the world. At the same time, a growing number of men have been looking within themselves and learning to open to their feelings and intuition.

I believe this is happening because we have reached a dead-end street with our "old world" relationships and externalized concepts of masculine and feminine. The old models and ways of doing things are too limiting for us now, and we have not yet evolved effective patterns to take their place. It's a period of chaos and confusion, pain and insecurity, but also of tremendous growth. We *are* making a leap into the new world. I believe that every form of relationship, from the most traditional marriage to homosexual or bisexual relationships, represents each person's attempt to find their feminine/masculine balance within.

Women have traditionally been in touch with their female energy but they haven't backed her up with their male energy. They have not acknowledged what they know inside. They have always acted as if they were powerless when they are really very powerful. They have gone after external validation (from men especially), rather than internally validating themselves for what they know and who they are.

Many women, like myself, have had strongly developed male energy but have used it in the "old male" way. I was very intellectual, very active, and drove myself very hard to shoulder the responsibilities of the world. I also had a very strongly developed female, but I didn't put her in charge. In fact, I ignored her a lot of the time. I basically protected my sensitive, vulnerable feelings by erecting a tough outer shell.

I've had to learn to take that powerful male energy and use it to listen to, trust, and support my female. This allows her the safety and support to emerge fully. I feel and appear softer, more receptive, and more vulnerable, but I am really much stronger than before.

Women are now learning to back themselves up and validate themselves, instead of abandoning the responsibility and trying to get a man to do it for them. However, it's a deep-seated pattern that has endured for centuries, and it takes time to change it in the deepest layers. The key is to just keep listening to, trusting, and acting on our deepest feelings.

The qualities that women have looked for in men — strength, power, responsibility, caring, excitement, romance — must be developed inside of ourselves. A simple formula is this: just treat yourself exactly the way you would want to be treated by a man!

The interesting thing is that what we create within us is always mirrored outside of us. This is the law of the universe. When you have built an inner male who supports and loves you, there will always be a man, or even many men, in your life who will reflect this. When you truly give up trying to get something outside yourself, you end up having what you always wanted!

For men, of course, the principle is exactly the same. Men are, traditionally, disconnected from their female energy, thereby disconnected from life, power, and love. They've been out there in the world secretly feeling helpless, alone, and empty, although they pretend to be in control and powerful. (War is a good example of the old male energy lacking the wisdom and direction of the female.) Men seek nurturing and internal connection through women but once they have connected with their own inner female, they will receive her incredible love from within themselves.

For men, all the qualities you've wanted from a woman — the nurturing, softness, warmth, strength, sexuality, and beauty — already exist in your inner female. You will feel this when you learn to listen to your inner feelings and support them. You need to totally respect and honor your inner female energy by acting on your feelings for her. Then every woman — every person — in your life will mirror that integration. They will have the qualities you've always wanted, and they will also receive love, warmth, nurturing, and strength from you.

Many men, especially in recent times, have chosen to connect deeply with their feminine energy and, in doing so, have disconnected from their male. They've rejected the old macho image and have no other concept of male energy to relate to. These men are usually so afraid of their male energy, fearing that it will burst forth with all the old mindlessness and violence they equate with maleness, that they reject the positive, assertive male qualities as well.

I feel it's very important for these men to embrace the concept of the new male — one who allows his spontaneous, active, aggressive male energy to flow freely, knowing that the power of his feminine is in charge, wisely directing him. This requires a deep trust that the inner female knows what she's doing and won't allow anything destructive or harmful to happen.

NEW WORLD RELATIONSHIPS

A new idea of relationships is emerging that is based on each person developing wholeness within him- or herself. Internally, each person is moving toward becoming a fully balanced feminine/masculine being with a wide range of expression, from softest receptivity to strongest action.

Externally, most people's style of expression will certainly be determined strongly by which type of body they are in — male or female.

When people hear these ideas they sometimes express the fear that we will all become outwardly androgynous — men and women all appearing pretty much the same. The reverse is actually true. The more women develop and trust their male aspect to support them and back them up internally, the safer they feel to allow their soft, receptive, beautiful feminine aspect to open up. The women I know who are going through this process (myself included) seem to become more feminine and beautiful even while they are strengthening their masculine qualities. Men who are surrendering and opening fully to their female energy are actually reconnected with the inner feminine power that enhances and strengthens their masculine qualities. Far from becoming effeminate, the men I know who are involved in this process become more secure in their maleness.

In the new world, when a man is attracted to a woman, he recognizes her as a mirror of his feminine aspect. Through her reflection he can learn more about his own female side and move through whatever fears and barriers he may have to come to a deeper integration within himself. When a woman falls in love with a man, she is seeing her own male reflected in him. In her interactions with him she can learn to strengthen and trust her masculine side.

If you know on a deep level that the person you're attracted to is a mirror of yourself, you cannot be overly dependent on him or her because you know that everything you see in your partner is also in you! You recognize that one of the main reasons you're in the relationship is to learn about yourself and deepen your connection with the universe. So, healthy relationships are based on the passion and excitement of sharing the journey into becoming a whole person.

This might sound as if we are evolving to a place where we are so whole within ourselves that we no longer need relationships at all! The paradox is this: as human beings, we are social, interdependent creatures. We *do* need one another.

Part of experiencing wholeness is accepting the parts of us that
need love, closeness, and intimacy with one another. So, creating conscious relationships involves honoring both our depen-
dence and our interdependence.

GAY RELATIONSHIPS

My own experience in relationships is heterosexual, so I can
hardly consider myself much of an expert on gay relationships. However, from talking and working with quite a few
gay and lesbian friends and clients, I do have a strong sense
that on a spiritual level, homosexual and bisexual relationships
are a powerful step that some beings take to break through
old, rigid roles and stereotypes to find their own truth.

For some people, being in a close, intense relationship
with a person or persons of the same sex is the most powerful mirroring process they can find. Two women, for example,
often seem to find a depth of connection with each other that
they don't find with a man. They use this intuitive feminine
connection to create a strong foundation and safe environment in which each can practice building their internal male.
They totally reflect and support each other in becoming whole
and balanced.

A man sometimes seems to find a matching male intensity
with another man — an ability to go all out that he wouldn't
find with a woman. He may also find in another man a support
for moving into and exploring his feminine self without feeling he has to fulfill the old, stereotyped male role.

I think many of these things are mysteries that we will

understand only in retrospect. I believe that every being chooses the life path and relationships that will help him or her to grow the fastest.

As we continue to evolve, I believe we will gradually stop categorizing ourselves and our relationships with any particular labels, such as gay, straight, and so on. I foresee a time when each person can be a unique entity with his or her free-flowing style of expression. Each relationship will be a unique connection between two beings, taking its individual form and expression. No categories are possible because each relationship is so different and follows its own flow of energy.

Exercise

Think of some of the most important women in your life. What are their strongest or most attractive qualities? Be aware that they mirror some aspects of your own female energy (whether you are a woman or a man).

Now think of some of the most important men in your life. What qualities do you most like, admire, or appreciate about them? Recognize that they reflect similar aspects of your own male energy (again, this applies to you whether you're a man or a woman).

If you have trouble seeing that some of the things you admire in others are in you as well, it may be because you have not yet developed those qualities in yourself as strongly as they have. In this case, try the following meditation.

Meditation

Get in a comfortable position. Close your eyes, relax, take a few deep, slow breaths, and move your consciousness into a deep, quiet place inside.

Bring to mind one person whom you admire or are attracted to. Ask yourself what qualities you find most attractive in this person. Do you see those same qualities in yourself? If not, try imagining that you possess those same qualities. Imagine how you would look, talk, and act. Picture yourself in a variety of situations and interactions.

If you feel these are qualities you want to further develop within yourself, continue to do this visualization regularly for a while.

Part Two

LIVING THE PRINCIPLES

Chapter Ten

TRUSTING INTUITION

*M*ost of us have been taught from childhood not to trust our feelings, not to express ourselves truthfully and honestly, not to recognize that at the core of our being lies a loving, powerful, and creative nature. We learn easily to try to accommodate those around us, to follow certain rules of behavior, to suppress our spontaneous impulses, and to do what is expected of us. Even if we rebel against this, we are trapped in our rebellion, doing the opposite of what we've been told in a knee-jerk reaction against authority. Very seldom do we receive any support for trusting ourselves, listening to our own sense of inner truth, and expressing ourselves in a direct and honest way.

When we consistently suppress and distrust our intuitive knowingness, looking instead for authority, validation, and approval from others, we give our personal power away. This leads to feelings of helplessness, emptiness, a sense of being a victim, and eventually anger and rage — and, if these feelings are also suppressed, to depression and deadness. We may simply succumb to these feelings and lead a life of quiet numbness. We may overcompensate for our feelings of powerlessness by attempting to control and manipulate other people and our environment. Or we may eventually burst forth with uncontrolled rage that is highly exaggerated and distorted by its long suppression. None of these are very positive alternatives.

The true solution is to re-educate ourselves to listen to and trust the inner truths that come to us through our intuitive feelings. Following our inner guidance may feel risky and frightening at first, because we are no longer playing it safe, doing what we "should" do, pleasing others, following rules, or deferring to outside authority. To live this way is to risk losing everything that we have held on to for reasons of external (false) security, but we will gain integrity, wholeness, true power, creativity, and the real security of knowing that we are in alignment with the power of the universe.

In suggesting that our intuition needs to be the guiding force in our lives, I am not attempting to disregard or eliminate the rational mind. The intellect is a very powerful tool, best used to support and give expression to our intuitive wisdom, rather than as we often use it — to suppress our intuition. Most of us have programmed our intellect to doubt our intuition. When an intuitive feeling arises, our rational minds immediately say, "I don't think that will work," "nobody else is doing it that way," or "what a foolish idea," and the intuition is disregarded.

As we move into the new world, it is time to re-educate our intellect to recognize the intuition as a valid source of information and guidance. We must train our intellect to listen to and express the intuitive voice. The intellect is by nature very disciplined and this discipline can help us to ask for and receive the direction of the intuitive self.

What does it mean to trust your intuition? How do you do it? It means tuning into your "gut feelings" — your deepest inner sense of personal truth — in any given situation, and acting on these feelings, moment by moment. Sometimes these "gut messages" may tell you to do something unexpected or inconsistent with your previous plans; they may require that you trust a hunch that seems illogical; you may feel more emotionally vulnerable than you are used to feeling; you may express thoughts, feelings, or opinions foreign to your usual beliefs; you may follow a dream or fantasy, or take some degree of financial risk to do something that feels important to you.

At first you may fear that trusting your intuition will lead you to do things that seem somewhat hurtful or irresponsible to others. For example, you may hesitate to break a date, even though you need time for yourself, because you fear hurting your date's feelings. I've found that when I really listen to and trust my inner voice, in the long run, everyone around me benefits as much as I do.

People may sometimes be temporarily disappointed, irritated, or a bit shaken up as you change your old patterns of relating to yourself and others. But this is usually because as you change, the people around you are automatically pushed to change as well. If you trust, you will see that the changes are also for their highest good. (If you do break that date, your friend may end up having a wonderful time doing something else.) If they don't want to change, they may move away from you, at least for a while; therefore, you must be willing to let go of the forms of relationship you have with people. If there is a deep connection between you, chances are good that you will be close again in the future. Meanwhile, everyone needs to grow in his or her own way and time. As you continue to follow your path, you will increasingly attract people who like you as you are and relate to you in a way that feels honest, supportive, and appreciative.

PRACTICING A NEW WAY OF LIVING

Learning to trust your intuition is an art form, and like all other art forms, it takes practice to perfect. You don't learn to do it overnight. You have to be willing to make "mistakes," to try something and fail, then try something different the next time — and sometimes, perhaps, even embarrass yourself or feel foolish. Your intuition is always correct, but it takes time to learn to hear it correctly. If you are willing to risk acting on what you believe to be true, and risk making mistakes, you will learn very fast by paying attention to what works and what doesn't. If you hold back out of fear of being wrong, learning to trust your intuition could take a lifetime.

It can be hard to distinguish the voice of our intuition from the many other selves that speak to us, from within — the different parts of ourselves that have their own idea of what's best for us.

People frequently ask me how to differentiate the voice or energy of intuition from all the others. Unfortunately, there's no simple, sure-fire way at first. Most of us are in touch with our intuition whether we know it or not, but we're actually in the habit of doubting or contradicting it so automatically that we don't even know it has spoken. The first step in learning is to pay more attention to what you feel inside, to the inner dialogue that goes on within you.

For example, you might feel, "I'd like to give Jim a call." Immediately, a rational, doubting voice inside says, "Why call him at this time of day? He probably won't be home," and you automatically ignore your original impulse to call. If you had called, you might have found him at home and discovered he had some important information for you.

Another example: you might get a feeling in the middle of the day that says, "I'm tired, I'd like to take a rest." You immediately think, "I can't rest now, I have a lot of work to do." So you drink some coffee to get yourself going and work the rest of the day. By the end of the day you feel tired, drained, and irritable, whereas if you had trusted your initial feeling, you might have rested for half an hour and continued about your tasks, refreshed and efficient, finishing your day in a state of balance.

As you become aware of this subtle inner dialogue between your intuition and your other inner voices, it's very important not to put yourself down or diminish this experience. Try to remain a somewhat objective observer. Notice what happens when you follow your intuitive feelings. The result is usually increased energy and power, and a sense of things flowing. Now notice what happens when you doubt, suppress, or act against your feelings. Usually, you will observe decreased energy; you may feel somewhat disempowered or depressed. You may even experience emotional or physical pain.

Whether or not you act on your intuitive feelings, you'll be learning something, so try not to condemn yourself when you don't follow your intuition (thus adding insult to injury!). Remember, it takes time to learn new habits; the old ways are deeply ingrained. I've been working intensively on my own re-education for many years, and while the results I'm enjoying are wonderful, there are still times when I don't yet have the courage or awareness to be able to trust myself completely and do exactly what I feel. I'm learning to be patient and compassionate with myself as I gain the courage to be true to myself.

Suppose you are trying to decide whether to change jobs. You might have a conservative self that feels it would be safest to stay where you are, an adventurous self that is eager to do something different, a self that is concerned about what other people will think, and so on. One way to handle this is to "listen" to each of these voices and write down what each has to say (perhaps using a different-colored pen for each one). Then just let yourself sit with all the conflicting viewpoints for a while without trying to resolve them or make a decision. Eventually, you will start to get an intuitive sense of what your next step needs to be.

As you get to know the different selves within you, you will discover that your intuitive self has an energy or a feeling that is different from the other voices. In time, you will learn to recognize it quite easily.

One important step in learning to hear and follow your intuition is simply to practice "checking in" regularly. At least twice a day, and much more often, if possible (once an hour is great), take a moment or two (or longer, if you can) to relax and listen to your gut feelings. Cultivate this habit of talking to your intuitive self. Ask for help and guidance when you need it and practice listening for answers that may come in many forms: words, images, feelings, or even through being led to some external source such as a book, a friend, or a teacher who will tell you just what you need to know. Your body is a tremendous helper in learning to follow your inner voice. Whenever you feel your body is in pain or discomfort, it is usually an indication that you have ignored your feelings. Use it as a signal to tune in and ask what you need to be aware of.

As you learn to live from your intuition, you give up making decisions with your head. You act moment by moment on what you feel and allow things to unfold as you go. In this way, you are led in the direction that is right for you, and decisions are made easily and naturally. If possible, try not to make big decisions concerning future events until you are clear about what you want. Focus on following the energy in the moment and you'll find that it will all be handled in its own time and way. When you must make a decision related to something in the future, follow your gut feeling about it at the time the decision needs to be made.

Remember, too, that although I sometimes speak of following your inner intuitive voice, most people do not literally experience it as a voice. Often it's more like a simple feeling, an energy, a sense of "I want to do this" or "I don't want to do that." Don't make it into a big deal, a mysterious mystical event, a voice from on high! It's a simple, natural human experience that we have lost touch with and need to reclaim.

The main sign that you are following your intuition in your life is increased aliveness. It feels like more life energy is flowing through your body. Sometimes it may even feel a little overwhelming, like more energy than your body can handle. You may even have the experience of feeling tired from too much energy coming through you. You won't bring through more energy than you can deal with, but it may stretch you a little! Your body's expanding its capacity to channel the universal energy. Relax into it and rest when you need to. Do things that help you stay grounded, such as physical exercise, being in nature, emotional self-nurturing, and eating healthy, substantial foods. Soon you'll feel more balanced and you'll even begin to enjoy the increasing intensity.

At first you may find that the more you act on your intuition, the more things in your life seem to be falling apart — you might lose your job, a relationship, or certain friends, or your car might even stop working! You're actually changing rapidly and shedding the things in your life that no longer fit. As long as you refused to let go of them, they imprisoned you. As you continue on this new path, following the energy moment by moment as best you can, you will see new forms begin to be created in your life — new relationships, new work, a new home, a new form of creative expression, or whatever. It will happen easily and effortlessly. Things will just fall into place, and doors will open in a seemingly miraculous way. You may have times when you will just go along, doing what you have energy to do, and not doing what you don't have energy to do, having a wonderful time, and you will, literally, be able to watch the universe creating through you. You're starting to experience the joy of being a creative channel!

SPECIFIC EXAMPLES

Here are a few examples from my life, and the lives of my friends and clients, of the types of situations you might be confronted with in following your intuition. Notice that the words in parentheses are the thoughts and feelings that might have held you back or stopped you from trusting your intuition in the past.

- Leaving a party or meeting because you realize you really don't want to be there (even though you're afraid of what others might think or you don't want to miss something good).
- Telling someone how you honestly feel (even though you're afraid of being rejected, and it makes you feel very vulnerable, and one part of you says, "You're just not supposed to do that").
- Deciding not to write your thesis because you really don't feel very interested in it; every time you think about it, it feels like a terrible chore (even though you spent five years working toward

it, and your parents will be upset if you don't get your degree, you'd really like to have the prestige, and you think you could get a better job with it).

- Taking singing lessons, music lessons, a dance class, or whatever interests you, because you have a fantasy that you would love to be able to sing, play an instrument, or dance (even though you don't think you have any talent, you're too old to learn now, or you might look foolish).

- Not going to work one day because you feel that you want a quiet day to yourself to hang around home, lie in the sun, take a walk, or even just lie in bed (even though you always go to work and think it's terribly irresponsible not to if you're not sick, or you're afraid you might lose your job, or you think it's silly or frivolous).

- Quitting your job because you hate it and you realize that you don't really need to do something that you don't like (even though you're not really sure what you're going to do next and you'll only have enough money to last you for a few months, and you feel scared about not having the security of a regular income).

- Not doing a favor for someone who's asked you to because you really don't want to and you know you'd feel resentful if you did (even though you're afraid you're selfish, or you might lose a friend or antagonize a co-worker).

- Spending a little money on something special for

yourself or someone else, on impulse, just because it makes you feel good (even though you're normally very frugal, and you really feel maybe you can't afford it).

- Telling someone your opinion about something because you're tired of pretending to agree with others (even though you normally wouldn't dare express yourself that way).

- Telling your family that you're not cooking dinner because you just don't feel like it (even though you're afraid you're being a bad wife and mother and they all might find out they don't need you anymore and your whole identity will be shot).

- Not making a decision about something because you're not sure yet how you really feel about it (even though it makes you feel uncomfortable and off balance to be in a state of indecisiveness).

- Starting your own business because you have a strong feeling inside that you can do it (even though you've never done anything like that before).

Well, you've got the idea. Trusting your intuition means tuning in as deeply as you can to the energy you feel, following that energy moment to moment, trusting that it will lead you where you want to go and bring you everything you desire. It means being yourself, being real and authentic in your communications, being willing to try new things because they feel right, and doing what turns you on.

HIGHLY INTUITIVE PEOPLE

Many people are already highly developed intuitively. Some are very much in touch with their intuition, but are afraid to act on it in the world. Often, these people will follow their intuitive promptings in one specific area of their lives, but not in others. Many artists, musicians, performers, and other highly creative people fall into this category. They strongly trust and spontaneously act on their intuition within the bounds of their art form; thus, they are extremely creative and often very productive, but they don't have the same degree of self-trust and willingness to back their feelings with action in other areas of their lives, particularly in their relationships and in matters of business and money. Thus, we have the classic case of the artistic type who is chaotic and unbalanced emotionally and/or inept or even exploited financially.

A classic example of this problem was seen in the movie *Lady Sings the Blues*, based on the life of the great singer Billie Holiday. In one scene, she is traveling with her show on a grueling tour of the country. She is feeling exhausted and depleted and yearns to go home to see her husband and to rest. She resolves to cancel her tour and follow her heart. However, her business managers succeed in convincing her that this move would ruin her career, that she must continue on the road. Shortly after giving in to their arguments, she begins to indulge heavily in drugs. From that point on, her life takes a downward and tragic course.

Naturally, one such incident does not ruin an entire life, but this movie provides a graphic illustration of the way many artists and performers give away their authority to other influences around them and suffer the resulting inner conflict, pain, and loss of power. In order to come into balance, these people must learn to trust their intuition and assert themselves in all areas of their lives.

Many psychics also experience this problem. They are very open, receptive, and intuitive, and do not block these qualities as many of us have done. They may even give their intuition free reign in their work or under certain conditions. Once again, they may not fully trust and back their intuition in every moment of their lives, especially in the area of personal relationships. They may be too wide open to other people's energies and often do not know how to stay connected to their own individual feelings and needs, how to assert themselves, and how to set boundaries. From my experience, these highly sensitive people often have problems with their bodies — either weight problems or chronic illness. These problems are healed when they learn to balance their receptive, intuitive nature (feminine energy) with an equally developed willingness to act on their feelings and assert themselves in personal relationships (masculine energy).

Many spiritual seekers who have spent a good deal of time meditating, becoming very sensitive and attuned to their energy, also have problems of imbalance. The seeker has a strong mental image of what it is to be "spiritual" — loving, open, and centered. He or she wants to act out this model at all times and thus is afraid to act spontaneously or express feelings honestly for fear that what comes out may be harsh, rude, angry, selfish, or unloving.

Since we are human, as we risk expressing ourselves more freely and honestly, some of what comes out will be unpolished, distorted, foolish, or thoughtless. As we learn to act on our inner feelings, all the ways in which we've blocked ourselves in the past are cleared out, and in that process, a lot of old "stuff" comes to the surface and is released. Many old beliefs and emotional patterns are brought to light and healed. In this process, we have to be willing to face and reveal our unconsciousness. (By the time we can see it, it's already changing anyway.) If we pretend to be more "together" than we really are, we will miss the opportunity to heal ourselves. I have found this to be a very vulnerable and out-of-control feeling. I can't worry too much about how I'm presenting myself or how I look to others or whether I'm doing the right thing. I just have to be myself as I am now, as best I can, accepting the mixture of enlightened awareness and human limitation that is what I am right now.

To be a creative channel, you just have to be real — be yourself. The more authentic, honest, and spontaneous you are, the more freely the creative force can flow through you. As it does so, it cleans out the remnants of old blockages. What comes out may sometimes be unpleasant or uncomfortable, but the energy moving through you will feel great! The more you practice this, the clearer you will become and the more alive you will feel.

Remember, too, that some of our spiritual models reflect our "good ideas" more than they reveal an accurate picture of enlightenment. The picture that many people have of wanting to be mellow, positive, and loving all the time is really an expression of their need to feel in control, good, and right. The universe has many colors, moods, speeds, styles, and direction; furthermore, they are all constantly changing. Only by letting go of some of our control and risking moving fearlessly with this flow will we get to experience the ecstasy of being a true channel.

Exercise

1. Write down all the reasons you can think of for not trusting and following your intuition. Include on the list any fears you have about what might happen to you if you trust your intuition and act on it all the time.

2. Review the meditation at the end of the third chapter ("Intuition"; see page 18).

3. At least twice a day (more often if you can remember), take a minute to relax, close your eyes, and "check in" with your gut feeling to see if you are doing what feels right, or if there's anything you need to be aware of.

4. For one day, or one week, assume that your intuitive feelings about things are always 100 percent right, and act as if that is so.

Chapter Eleven

FEELINGS

*O*ne of the most common problems I encounter in my work is that so many people are out of touch with their feelings. When we have suppressed and closed off our feelings, we cannot contact the universe within us, we cannot hear our intuitive voice, and we certainly can't enjoy being alive.

It seems that many people did not get enough real emotional support when they were growing up. Our parents didn't know how to support their own feelings, much less ours. Perhaps they were too overwhelmed with the difficulties and responsibilities in their lives to be able to give us the emotional response and care we needed.

Whatever the causes, if we don't feel anyone is there to listen to us and care about our feelings, or if we get a negative response when we do express ourselves, we soon learn to suppress our emotions. When we bottle up our feelings, we close off the life energy flowing through our bodies. The energy of these unfelt, unexpressed feelings remains blocked in our bodies, causing emotional and physical discomfort and eventually illness and disease. We become numb and somewhat deadened.

In every workshop I give, I encounter people who have been repressing their feelings throughout their lives. Many people are afraid to feel their so-called negative emotions — sadness, hurt, anger, fear, despair. They are afraid that if they open up to experiencing these feelings, the emotions will be overwhelming. They are terrified that if they get into the experience, they'll remain stuck forever.

In fact, the opposite is true. When you are willing to fully experience a particular feeling, the blocked energy releases quickly and the feeling dissolves. When counseling someone who has blocked emotion, I support them in moving into the feeling and allowing it to overwhelm them. Once they've felt it completely and expressed it, it usually dissipates within a few minutes. It's amazing to watch people who have suppressed a painful feeling for thirty, forty, or fifty years release it within a few minutes and experience peace in its place. (It may be important to have the support of a therapist or support group during this process.)

Once you have experienced and released blocked emotion from the past, a greater flow of energy and vitality will enrich your life. It is important to learn to be in touch with your feelings as they arise: in this way, they can continue to move through and your channel will remain clear.

Emotions are cyclical in nature and, like the weather, they

are constantly changing. In the course of an hour, a day, or a week we may move through a wide range of feelings. If we understand this, we can learn to enjoy all our feelings and simply allow them to keep changing. But when we are afraid of certain feelings, like sadness or anger, we put on our emotional brakes when we start to feel them. We don't want to feel the emotion completely, so we get stuck halfway into it and never get through it.

Often people come to my workshops who want to learn how to "think positively" so they won't feel so stuck in their negative feelings. They are surprised when I urge them to feel more of their negative feelings, not fewer! It's only by loving and accepting all parts of ourselves that we can be free and fulfilled.

We tend to think of certain feelings as "painful" and therefore wish to avoid them. The experience of pain, however, is actually resistance to a sensation. Pain is a mechanism in our physical body that helps us avoid physical harm or notifies us that a part of us has been injured and needs care. If you touch a hot stove, you will feel pain; this is resistance to the sensation of heat that you are experiencing. It causes you to pull your hand away and thus avoid damaging your body. If you do touch something hot for too long and burn yourself, the subsequent pain lets you know that your body needs healing.

So, on the physical level, pain is a useful mechanism in that it lets us know that we are in danger. However, if a sensation isn't really dangerous, you can relax into it and the pain will diminish and dissolve. For example, if you stretch a muscle farther than usual, it will at first feel painful, but as you continue to relax gently and steadily into the stretched position, the pain will be released. In childbirth, if a woman resists the intense sensation she is experiencing, she will have great pain. The more she is able to relax into the sensation, the less painful it will be.

On the emotional level, it is our resistance to a feeling that causes us pain. If, because we are afraid of a certain feeling, we suppress it, we will experience emotional pain. If we allow ourselves to feel it and accept it fully, it becomes an intense sensation, though not a painful one.

There are no such things as "negative" or "positive" feelings — we make them negative or positive by our rejection or acceptance of them. To me, all feelings are part of the wonderful, ever-changing sensation of being alive. If we love all the different feelings we experience, they become so many rainbow colors of life.

Here are some emotions that people seem to be most afraid of, with a suggestion of one way you might handle them:

Fear: It's important to acknowledge and accept your fears. If you accept yourself for feeling afraid, and don't try too hard to push past your fears, you will start to feel more secure, and the fear will lessen. Take risks when you feel ready to do so, but don't force yourself to do things you aren't ready for yet.

Sadness: Sadness is related to the opening of your heart. If you allow yourself to feel sad, especially if you can cry, you will find that your heart opens further and you can feel more love. If possible, reach out for comfort and support from someone who accepts you and your sadness and can just be with you.

Grief: This is an intense form of sadness, related to the death or ending of something. It is our way of releasing the old so that we can be open to the new. It is very important to allow yourself to grieve fully and not to cut this process short. Grief comes in waves, at first close together, then, gradually, farther apart. Grief can sometimes last a long time, or recur periodically for a very long time. It's necessary to accept it and give yourself as much support as you need to get through it, whenever it comes up.

Hurt: Hurt is an expression of vulnerability. We tend to mask it with defensiveness and blame so we won't have to admit how vulnerable we really feel. It's important to express feelings of hurt directly and, if possible, in a nonblaming way (in other words: "I felt really hurt when you didn't ask me to go with you," as opposed to "You don't care about my feelings. How could you be so insensitive," and so on).

Hopelessness: This can be the result of not trusting ourselves, honoring our feelings and needs, or taking proper care of ourselves. We may need to be more true to ourselves and more assertive. Hopelessness can also be a stage we go through when we are letting go of our old patterns of control, and learning to surrender to our higher power.

Anger: When we disown our true power and allow other people to have undue power over us, we become angry. Usually we suppress this anger and go numb. As we start to get back in touch with our power, the first thing we feel is the stored-up anger. So for many people who are growing more conscious, it's a very positive sign when they begin to get in touch with their anger. It means they are reclaiming their power.

If you have not allowed yourself to get angry much in your life, you will start to set up situations and people that trigger your anger. Don't focus too much on the external problem when this happens; just allow yourself to feel the anger and recognize that it is your power. Visualize a volcano going off inside of you and filling you with power and energy.

Often people are very frightened of their anger — they fear it will cause them to do something harmful. If you have this fear, see if you can create a safe situation where you can allow yourself to feel it fully and express it — either alone, or with a therapist or support group. Allow yourself to rant and rave, kick and scream, throw a temper tantrum, throw or hit pillows — whatever you feel like doing. Once you've done this in a safe environment (you may need to do it regularly), you will no longer be so afraid of doing something destructive and you will be able to handle the situations in your life more effectively.

If you are a person who has felt and expressed a lot of anger in your life, you need to look for the hurt that is underneath it and express that. You are probably using anger as a defense mechanism to avoid being vulnerable.

An important key in transforming anger into an acceptance of your power is learning to assert yourself. Learn to ask for what you want and do what you want to do without being unduly influenced by other people. When you stop giving your power away to other people, you won't feel angry anymore.

Acceptance of your feelings is directly related to becoming a creative channel. If you don't allow your feelings to flow, your channel will be blocked. If you've stored up a lot of emotions, you have a lot of blocked energy or erupting emotions inside of you which don't allow you to hear the more subtle voice of your intuition.

Often people need help in experiencing and releasing old emotional blocks and learning to live in a more *feeling* way. If you believe you need some help with this, find a good counselor, therapist, or support group. In seeking a therapist, ask people you know for referrals and don't hesitate to interview several until you find one that you like. Try to find one who seems to be in touch with his or her own feelings, relates to you in a real and honest way, and supports you in experiencing and expressing your own feelings, and in trusting yourself.

Whether you seek professional help or not, make a practice of asking yourself frequently throughout the day how you are feeling. Try to learn to distinguish between what you are thinking and how you are feeling (many people have difficulty with this). As much as possible, accept and enjoy your feelings, and you will find that they open the door to a rich, full, and passionate life.

Exercise

When you wake up in the morning, close your eyes and put your attention in the middle of your body — your heart, your solar plexus, and your abdomen. Ask yourself how you are feeling emotionally right now. Try to distinguish your feelings from the thoughts you are having in your head. Are you feeling peaceful, excited, anxious, sad, angry, joyful, frustrated, guilty, loving, lonely, fulfilled, serious, playful?

If there seems to be an anxious or upset feeling inside of

you, go into that feeling and give it a voice. Ask it to talk to you and tell you what it's feeling. Make an effort to hear it and listen to its point of view. Be sympathetic, loving, and supportive toward your feelings. Ask what you can do to take care of yourself at this time.

Repeat this exercise before you go to sleep at night, and at any other time during the day that feels appropriate.

Chapter Twelve

BALANCING BEING AND DOING

To follow our inner guidance, we must be open to a full range of experiences. We must also learn to trust what messages we are receiving. If the message is to move forward, then we trust the universe will take care of us and we will be provided for. If we don't have clarity, or we receive a message to pause, then we trust that the answers will be revealed and practice becoming comfortable with the unknown. We will always be pushed by our inner guidance to explore aspects of ourselves that are less developed, to express and experience ourselves in new ways. If we ignore these inner impulses, we will be forced by external life circumstances to explore the opposite polarities from the ones we are most comfortable with. One way or another, our higher self makes sure that we get the message of what we have to do. At times we may swing from one polarity to the other until we come into balance.

You can expect that your intuition will lead you in directions that are new and different for you. If you are comfortable in one type of personality or pattern, you will probably be asked to start expressing the opposite. It's good to know this, especially when you're in the process of learning to hear your inner guidance. A good rule might be to "expect the unexpected."

One of the most important sets of polarities that we need to develop and balance is the polarity between the being and doing energies. Most of us are more identified with one of these energies and disown the other.

The two types could be called the "doers" and the "be-ers." They roughly correspond to "type A" and "type B" personalities in common psychological terminology.

The doers are people who are primarily action oriented. They know how to get things done, and they usually aren't afraid to put themselves out there and take risks in expressing themselves or trying new things. Basically, they are good at expressing their outgoing energy. They have trouble receiving. They don't like feeling vulnerable. The most difficult thing for them is doing nothing — not being engaged in some type of constructive activity. Unstructured time makes them uncomfortable and they usually fill it up with lots of activity. They tend to be driven and have a hard time really relaxing. Their male, active energy is more developed, and they may be somewhat uncomfortable with their female, receptive side.

Be-ers are mainly oriented toward inner attunement. They

know how to relax and take it easy. They enjoy the subtle pleasure of life and often know how to nurture themselves and others, and how to play. They are usually flexible and are happy to "hang out" with unstructured time. They may have trouble with action. They fear putting themselves out in new or unusual ways and tend to hold back a lot. They aren't very assertive and sometimes have trouble expressing feelings or opinions. They worry about what others will think of them. They may be uncomfortable in the world and lack the confidence to deal with people, business, money, and so on. Their female, receptive energy is more developed and they may be uncomfortable or distrustful of their male, outgoing side.

If you are primarily a doer, your intuition will almost surely lead you in the direction of doing less. Your feelings will tell you to stop, to relax and take a day off (or a week, or six months!), to spend more time alone with yourself, to spend time in nature, to spend time with no plan and no list, and just practice following the energy as you feel it. If you consistently ignore these inner messages to slow down, you may develop a minor or major illness. This may be the way the universe forces you to become more balanced.

The hardest thing for a doer is getting no message at all, having to hang out and wait and "do nothing" until further guidance comes. I am primarily a doer, a list maker, a very active person, and one of the hardest things for me has been when the universe has forced me to do nothing! Yet I find that those times are the most powerful and inspirational of all because that's when I can really stop long enough to feel my spirit. In fact, I finally realized and had to admit that I kept busy all my life in order to avoid feeling that power. I was afraid of "empty" time and space because it was actually so full of the universal force.

If you are more comfortable with being you will undoubtedly be pushed by your inner self into more action, more expression, more risk taking in the world. The key for you is to follow your impulses and to try doing things you wouldn't normally do on impulse. You don't have to know why you're doing something or see any particular result from it at first. It's important to simply practice acting spontaneously on your feelings, especially when it comes to dealing with people, expressing your creative energy in the world, making money, or anything else you might normally avoid. Don't push yourself harder or farther than you are ready to go. It's very important to respect your own boundaries and rhythms for growing. Make sure the voice isn't coming from your inner authoritarian self, saying, "You *should* put yourself out in this way." (If it's a *should*, it's seldom the voice of the universe.) Rather, follow the feelings you have that guide you to practice expressing yourself and building your confidence in a supportive way.

Meditation

Get comfortable and close your eyes. Take a few deep breaths, and each time you exhale, relax your body and mind into a deep, quiet level of consciousness. Imagine yourself as a very balanced person. You are able to relax, play, and nurture yourself frequently, and you enjoy having time and space in your life when there is nothing special you have to do. Yet you act on your feelings and impulses spontaneously, express yourself strongly and directly, and risk trying new things whenever you are inspired to do so. You live in the full range of being and doing, so you can follow your inner guidance in whatever direction it leads you.

Exercise

If you are primarily a doer, spend one day consciously doing as little as possible. Take note of how you feel and what happens.

If you are better at being than doing, take a day to practice acting on any impulse or inspiration you have, without expecting any particular results. Try several new and unusual things, especially things that involve making contact with people or putting yourself out in the world in new ways. Notice how you are feeling before, while, and after you do this.

Chapter Thirteen

AUTHORITARIAN AND REBEL

*T*he authoritarian and the rebel are two parts of the personality that many of us have in one form or another. If they are strong voices in us, they can make it difficult to sense and follow our intuition. If we are unconscious of them, they may control our behavior in a way that interferes with our ability to get in touch with our true desires. The battle between them can create tremendous conflict within us, as well.

As in dealing with all of our inner selves, the first and most important step is becoming conscious of them. Once we become aware of them, we are already separating from being identified with them. We recognize them as part of us, and we begin to have conscious choice about how much power we give them. We can appreciate them for the ways in which they've tried to help us, and for what they still have to offer us.

The inner authoritarian carries our need for order and structure and the rules we have learned about how we should behave. People who grow up in a home with a strong authoritarian parent figure, or in a very authoritarian religion, always develop a powerful inner authoritarian self who carries all the values and rules of the external authority figures. It tries to protect you and keep you safe by making sure that you follow the rules, maintain order, and behave as a good, responsible person.

If you have a strong authoritarian self, you usually make one of two choices: you strive to follow its rules or you rebel against them. If you follow them faithfully, you are likely to be a responsible, law-abiding person and oftentimes a high achiever. You may, however, lose touch with your spontaneous, free-spirited, creative energies, and eventually you may even feel that you've lost your soul.

Some people react to their authoritarian upbringing and their own internalized authoritarian by developing a strong rebellious self. They become identified with the rebel and disown the authoritarian self, but it remains in the shadow of their unconscious, trying to control their behavior and constantly triggering the rebel into action.

The rebel usually develops in childhood or adolescence, in an attempt to maintain a sense of self and find some freedom in an overly oppressive rule structure. This can literally be a life saver at the time. Unfortunately, the rebel is just a knee-jerk reaction to the authoritarian's rules. It reacts in rebellion to any controlling influence from inside or out. It will automatically do the opposite of whatever it thinks it's supposed to do.

Thus, it is really no freer than the authoritarian; it's just the flip side of the same coin. It has little to do with the person's true desires; it just does the opposite of what it's told. Eventually, it becomes a self-sabotaging force, often inclined toward addictive and self-destructive behavior.

Many people who identify with the rebel were the "black sheep" of their families, acting out the disowned energies of the other family members. They may continue this pattern in later life, always becoming the scapegoat or shadow carrier in every relationship.

The rebel will fight against any energy it fears will control it, including legitimate authority figures, or your own internal attempts to create positive structure in your life. For example: your boss might make a reasonable request, and you become angry and resist doing what she asks; you decide to eat a healthier diet and your rebel immediately eats three pieces of chocolate cake; you decide to exercise in the morning and you find you've slept until noon.

As always, when we are overly identified with an energy, we attract its opposite in our relationships. If you are identified with your authoritarian voice, you will probably have a rebellious mate, rebellious children, and/or rebellious employees. If you are identified with the rebel, you will constantly attract authoritarian energies into your life — the police, the IRS, your mate, your boss, etc.

Whether we become overly identified with the authoritarian or with the rebel, these identifications are unconscious, so there is no real choice or freedom. When your authoritarian self is dictating your every move, or is constantly battling with your rebel, it is almost impossible to get in touch with your intuitive feelings or true desires.

The key, then, is to become aware of and learn to recognize both of these energies. Try to notice when one or the other takes over, or when they are locked in conflict. Once you become aware of them, acknowledge them for trying to help and protect you. Then see if you can drop in a little deeper to intuitively sense what it is that you really need and want in this situation.*

A client of mine was frustrated with her career and saw that she was bringing about her firing. She was working in an office, doing administrative work for a salesperson. Although she had great organizational abilities, she found herself forgetting to do things. Her boss would come to her and remind her of what hadn't been done and she would fume with anger. She realized she was getting angry anytime her boss told her to do something, however reasonable. She felt she could not afford to lose the job, but she did not want to stay there either. She felt trapped. As we talked, she started to identify the rebel side of herself. She saw she was fighting with the authoritarian, who said she had to stay at that job, and against her boss, who was in a "controlling" position. She went back to her childhood and examined when she had first developed a rebel

---

* The best way that I have found to become conscious of the different selves within us and work with them is the Voice Dialogue technique of Hal and Sidra Stone (see Recommended Resources).

inside. She saw that she'd had trouble with authorities at other jobs and in school. She realized she was being triggered by old patterns.

When she saw this, she immediately wanted to change these parts of herself. I explained to her that she could not force change. If she tried to change or fix her rebel, she'd be activating it, and the rebel would continue to fight. She needed to become willing to watch herself react, to accept that this was the pattern she was acting out. Once she had really grasped what I was saying to her, I asked her to close her eyes and drop into a deeper place inside herself. She needed to ask her intuition what she really wanted.

It turned out she wanted to be a saleswoman, but was afraid to try. She was growing angry at herself for sitting behind a desk when she knew there was something else she was meant to do.

After realizing what she wanted to do, she was able to come up with several steps she could take to support her goal. She decided to keep her job for the interim and enlist her boss's help in her goal. She decided to conduct several informational interviews at sales companies to get ideas of places she might want to work. Having seen clearly what she wanted and discussed the action she could take to help herself, she felt much better.

A month later she called me and said that although her authoritarian and rebel continue to fight it out, they seemed to have less power. She had continued to support her goal to do sales work and was feeling much better about her life and less reactive to her boss.

Exercise

Identify some of your rules and behaviors that feel demanding and controlling (overly authoritarian) to you. Use the categories below, in addition to any of your own. I have given some examples in each category.

Work: *I must work forty to sixty hours per week; I must work hard to get anywhere; I can't make money doing what I want.*

Money: *I'm never going to have enough money; I must save money in case something happens; I must not be frivolous with money.*

Relationships: *I have to find a mate; I must please my mate; I have to be monogamous; I'd better be satisfied with what I've got.*

Sex: *I have to have an orgasm every time I have sex; I have to be in love with someone to have sex; I have to be the greatest, most sensual lover.*

Now write down any corresponding rebel thoughts you may have. For example, *Who needs work; I'm going to quit my job*; or *Who cares about money anyway, I don't need it*; or *I'll just do what I want behind my mate's back.*

After you've written out the authoritarian and rebel dialogues, drop into a deeper place and ask yourself what you most want; discover what is true for you. Write down any thoughts or feelings that come to you.

Chapter Fourteen

RELATIONSHIPS

Relationships in the old world have often had a primarily external focus — we try to make ourselves whole and happy by getting something from outside ourselves. Inevitably, this expectation results in disappointment, resentment, and frustration. Either these feelings build up constantly and cause continual strife or they are suppressed and lead to emotional numbness. Still, we cling to relationships out of emotional insecurity, or go from one to another searching for that missing piece that we haven't yet found.

We've been in this tragic predicament for at least a few thousand years; now we seem to be approaching a crisis point. Relationships and families as we've known them seem to be falling apart at a rapid rate. Many people are panicky about this; some try to re-establish the old traditions and value systems in order to cling to a feeling of order and stability in their lives.

It's useless to try to go backward, however, because our consciousness has already evolved beyond the level where we were willing to make the sacrifices necessary to live that way. In the past, many people were willing to hang on to an essentially dead relationship for an entire lifetime because it gave them physical and emotional stability.

Now more and more of us are realizing that it is possible to have deeper intimacy and ongoing aliveness and passion in a relationship. We're willing to let go of old ideas about relationship in order to search for these ideals, but we don't know where to find them. Many of us are still looking outside ourselves, sure that if we just find the right man or woman to be with, we'll be blissfully happy — or thinking that if only our kids or our parents would behave the right way, then we'd be fine. We're confused and frustrated, our relationships seem to be in chaos, and we don't have the old traditions to lean on or anything new to take their place. Yet we can't go back; we must move forward into the unknown to create new kinds of relationships.

In order to do this, it's important to understand that our external relationships reflect our internal relationships with ourselves. My primary relationship is my relationship with myself — all others are mirrors of it. As I learn to love myself, I automatically receive the love and appreciation that I desire from others. If I am committed to myself and to living my truth, I will attract others with equal commitment. My willingness to be intimate with my own deep feelings creates the space for intimacy with another. Enjoying my own company allows me to have fun with whomever I'm with. And feeling the aliveness and power of the universe flowing through me creates a life of passionate feeling and fulfillment that I share with anyone I'm involved with.

TAKING CARE OF OURSELVES

Because many of us have never really learned how to take good care of ourselves, our relationships have been based on trying to get someone else to take care of us.

As babies, we are very aware and intuitive. From the time we are born, we perceive our parents' emotional pain and neediness, and we immediately begin to develop the habit of trying to please them and fulfill their needs so that they will continue to take care of us.

Later on, our relationships continue along the same lines. There is an unconscious telepathic agreement: "I'll try to do what you want me to do and be the person you want me to be if you will be there for me, give me what I need, and not leave me."

This system doesn't work very well. Other people are seldom able to fulfill our needs consistently or successfully, so we get disappointed and frustrated. Then either we try to change the other people to better suit our needs (which never works) or we resign ourselves to accept less than we really want. Furthermore, when we're trying to give other people what they want, we almost invariably do things we don't really want to do and end up resenting them, either consciously or unconsciously.

At this point, we may realize that it doesn't work to try to take care of ourselves by taking care of others. I'm the only one who can actually take good care of me, so I might as well do it directly and allow others to do the same thing for themselves. This doesn't mean we can't care for and give to others; it just means that we make a conscious choice to give or not, based on what we truly feel rather than out of fear or obligation. In fact, the better we take care of ourselves, the more we have to give.

What does it mean to take care of yourself? For me, it means trusting and following my intuition. It means taking time to listen to all my feelings — including the feelings of the child within me that is sometimes hurt or scared — and responding with care, love, and appropriate action. It means putting my most important inner needs first and trusting that as I do this, everyone else's needs will get taken care of, and everything that needs to be done will get handled.

For example, if I'm feeling sad, I might crawl into bed and cry, taking time to be very loving and nurturing to myself. Or I might find someone caring to talk to until some of the feelings are released and I feel lighter.

I'm learning to put the work aside if I've been working too hard, no matter how important it seems, and take some time to play, or just to take a hot bath and read a novel.

I'm learning to say no as clearly and lovingly as possible if someone I love wants something from me that I truly don't want to give, and trust that he or she will actually be better off than if I did it when I didn't want to. This way, when I say yes, I really mean it.

There is a very important point I want to make here — it

concerns something I was confused about for a long time and finally understood. Taking care of yourself does not mean "doing it all alone." Creating a good relationship with yourself is not done in a vacuum, without relationship to other people. If it were, we could all become hermits for a few years until we had a perfect relationship with ourselves, and then just emerge and suddenly have perfect relationships with others.

It is important that we be able to be alone, of course, and some people do need to withdraw from outside relationships to a certain degree, until they feel really comfortable with themselves. Sooner or later, though, we need the reflection that a relationship offers us. We need to build and strengthen our relationship with ourselves in the world of form through interaction with other people.

The difference in these approaches is the focus. In the old world of relationships, the focus was on the other person and on the relationship itself. We communicated for the purpose of trying to get the other person to understand us and give us more of what we needed. In new world relationships, the focus is on building our relationship with ourselves and the universe. We communicate to keep our channel clear and to give ourselves more of what we need. The words we speak may even be the same, but the energy is different, and so is the result.

For example, suppose I'm feeling lonely and want my partner to spend the evening with me although I know that he is planning to do something else. Previously, I might have been afraid to ask for what I wanted directly. I probably would have stayed home alone and focused on learning to enjoy being alone. Later when I talked with him, I would feel some resentment, though I wouldn't admit it, to either myself or him. Nevertheless, he would feel this resentment and become guilty and resentful toward me. None of this would come out in the open until later when we were having an argument and I might say, "Well you don't care about my feelings anyway; you never want to be with me." At this point, I'm communicating to him, telepathically, my underlying feeling that he is responsible for my happiness.

Now (hopefully), I would be more direct from the beginning. I'd say, "I know you have other plans, but I'm feeling a need for connection right now and I would love it if you would spend the evening with me." I'm taking responsibility for asking for what I want, and in doing so, I'm actually taking care of myself even though I'm asking for something from him. The key here is that my focus is on myself — this is what I'm feeling and this is what I want. I have to be willing to make myself vulnerable to do this. But I have found that it is the willingness to say what I feel and want that makes me feel whole. In a sense, I'm already feeling more fulfilled because I was willing to back myself up.

Everything is out in the open, and he's free to respond honestly. Hopefully, he will check inside to find out what's true for him. If he wants to fulfill my request, that's icing on the cake! If he doesn't, I may feel sad or hurt. I'll communicate my feelings (again, I'm doing it for my own sake, to keep myself clear) and then let go. I'll use that evening as a time to go deeper within myself and strengthen my connection with the universe.

I've found a very interesting thing. When I communicate truthfully and directly, in a nonblaming, nonjudgmental way, and say everything I really want to say, it doesn't seem to matter so much how the other person responds. They may not do exactly what I want, but I feel so clear and empowered from taking care of myself that it's easier to let go of the result. If I keep being honest and vulnerable with my feelings to my partner, family, and friends, I won't end up with hidden needs or resentment.

When you take care of yourself this way, more often than not, you do get what you ask for. If not, the next step is to let go. Go inside yourself and tune in to what your intuition is telling you to do next. Always let it take you to a deeper connection with yourself and the universe.

Thus, an important part of creating a loving relationship with yourself is to acknowledge your needs and to learn to ask for what you want. We're afraid to do this because we're afraid to appear too needy. It's the hidden, unacknowledged needs, however, that cause us to seem too needy. They aren't coming out directly so they come out indirectly or telepathically. People feel them and back away from us because they intuitively know they can't help us if we aren't acknowledging our need for help!

It's paradoxical that as we recognize and acknowledge our own needs and ask for help directly, we are actually becoming stronger. It's the male within supporting the female. People find it easy to give to us, and we feel more and more whole.

FOLLOWING ENERGY

I have found that when I'm willing to trust and follow my energy, it leads me into relationships with the people from whom I have the most to learn. The stronger the attraction (or reaction), the stronger the mirror. So the energy will always lead me to the most intense learning situation.

It can be frightening at first to try to live this way. We have always been terrified to trust our own feelings, especially in the realm of relationships and sexuality. Because this energy is so intense, so changeable and unpredictable, we fear that utter chaos will reign. We're terrified of being hurt or hurting someone else. We don't trust that the universe knows what it's doing, or else we don't trust ourselves to be able to accurately follow our inner guidance. And there's good reason for this. In the area of relationships, we have so many old patterns and addictions that it is often difficult to accurately hear our intuitive inner voice.

Following your energy does not mean acting out every impulse, feeling, or fantasy that you have — that would be the road to chaos. In order to follow your energy constructively, it's important to be aware of the various selves or voices within you, which may at times have conflicting feelings and needs. Through this kind of awareness, you can begin to sense the deeper intuitive feeling of where the life force is trying to take you, while honoring important agreements, boundaries, and commitments you may have with others.

Until now, most of us have avoided dealing with our fears by constructing stringent rule structures for all our relationships. Every relationship is fitted into a certain category, and each category has a list of rules and appropriate behaviors attached to it. This person is a friend, so I behave this way; this person is my husband, so he is supposed to do these things; this person is in my family, so this is how we act with each other; and so on. There's very little space left to discover the truth of each relationship.

Some people rebel against these rule systems and purposely create relationships that go counter to our established cultural norms — sometimes this is the case with nonmonogamous relationships, homosexual and bisexual relationships, and so on. If motivated mainly by rebellion, these relationships may be largely reactions against the rules and still may not involve a true attunement to our real needs.

Just as every being is a unique entity, unlike anyone else, every connection between two or more beings is also unique. No relationship is exactly like any other. Furthermore, the nature of the universe is constant change. People change all the time and so do relationships.

So when we try too hard to label and control relationships, we destroy them. Then we spend a lot of time and energy fruitlessly trying to bring them to life again.

We must be willing to let our relationships reveal themselves to us. If we tune into ourselves, trust ourselves, and express ourselves fully and honestly with each other, the relationship will unfold in its own unique and fascinating way. Each relationship is an amazing adventure; you never know exactly where it will lead. It keeps changing its mood, flavor, and form from minute to minute, day by day, year to year. At times, it may take you closer to each other. At other times, it may take you farther apart.

COMMITMENT AND INTIMACY

When we discuss the idea of trusting and following our energy, people often ask where the concept of commitment fits into this picture.

Because we have been so focused on externals, most of us have attempted to make a commitment to an external relationship. What we are really committing to is a certain set of rules — "I agree to behave in such and such a manner so that we can feel secure about this relationship." Usually these rules are not spelled out clearly; they are assumed. People say they are in a committed relationship but seldom clarify to themselves, or each other, what exactly they are committed to doing or not doing.

Generally, in a romantic relationship, one assumption is that the partners are agreeing not to have sex with anyone else. Even that is rather vague, though, as no one defines what "having sex" is. Often the implied agreement is not to feel sexual attraction toward anyone else. Yet how can you make an agreement not to feel something? Feelings aren't under our conscious control. We can make commitments about how we will behave, since we do have conscious control of our actions. Most people find that a commitment to monogamous behavior is a necessity in order to preserve the sense of intimacy they desire in a primary relationship. The important question is, do we make that commitment as a way of controlling our partner ("I'll be monogamous so that you will have to be, too") or from our own integrity ("I choose to be monogamous because I want the depth of intimacy that it will create in my primary relationship").

The real problem with many of the commitments we make or assume is that they don't allow room for the inevitable changes and growth of people and relationships. If you promise to behave by a certain set of rules that come from outside of you, eventually you are going to have to choose between being true to yourself and being true to those rules. When you stop being honest and real, there's not much left of you to be in the relationship. You end up with an empty shell — a nice commitment, but no real people in it!

Because this type of commitment attempts to keep the *form* of the relationship from changing, more often than not, it simply doesn't last. The fact is that relationships *do* change form and no commitment can guarantee that they won't. No external form can give us the security that we seek. You could be married for fifty years and in the fifty-first year your spouse could decide to leave you!

If we only realize this, it can save us so much pain. People who divorce almost inevitably feel that they have failed, because they assume all marriages should last forever. In many cases, however, the marriage has actually been a success — it's helped each person to grow to the point where they no longer need the same form.

What causes the pain in many cases is that we don't know how to allow the form to change *while still honoring the underlying love and connection.* When you are deeply involved with another human being, the soul connection often lasts forever. The intensity of energy in the relationship, however, increases or decreases in accordance with how much there is to be learned from it at any given time. When you've learned a great deal from being with someone, the energy between you may eventually diminish to the point where you no longer need to interact on a personality level as much, or at all. Sometimes, the energy renews itself again later on another level.

We don't understand this, so we feel guilty, disappointed, and hurt when our relationships change form. We don't really know how to share our feelings effectively with each other, and so we often respond to these feelings by cutting off our connection with the other person. This causes us real pain, because we are actually cutting off our own deep feelings. I have found that changes in relationships can be less painful, and at times even beautiful, when we can communicate honestly and trust ourselves in the process.

Most people believe that sacrifice and compromise are necessary in order to preserve a relationship. The need to sacrifice and compromise is based on a misunderstanding of the nature of the universe. We fear that there is not enough love for us and that the truth may be hurtful. In fact, the universe is filled with love, and the truth, when we can see it, is always healing.

When I'm willing to be honest and ask for what I want, to continue sharing my feelings openly, I find that the underlying truth in any situation is the same for all concerned. At first it may seem that I want one thing and the other person wants something else. If we both keep telling the truth as we feel it, sooner or later it works out so that we both see that we can have what we truly want.

For example, a couple who are clients of mine were experiencing a great deal of conflict about their work. They were partners is a very successful business. She was tired of the business and wanted to do something else. He loved the work and wanted to continue but did not want to do it without her. They fought constantly about whether to sell the business (her desire) or continue and expand it (his desire).

Once they began to communicate on a deeper level, they uncovered their fears. She yearned to express herself creatively in new ways, but was terrified that she would not be able to successfully step out on her own without his constant support. She was also afraid that she would not be able to make as much money, and he would feel resentful about her diminished contribution to the family income. He was afraid that he would be unable to handle the business successfully without her; he depended heavily on her creative input and did not trust his own intuitive capacity. Also, he feared that his working life would be dull and drab without her warmth and humor.

Having expressed their feelings fully, they were able to see that they were both at the point of making a leap into a new level of independence and creativity. They were ready to let go of some of their dependency on each other and develop more trust in themselves. She gradually withdrew from the business and started a new and very different career, which she ultimately found very exciting and rewarding. He continued to run the business and developed it in new and interesting directions. Their relationship was enhanced by their increased independence and self-confidence.

For me, commitment in relationship needs to be based on a commitment to myself — to love, honor, obey, and cherish my own being. My commitment in relationship is to respect my own truth and do my best to honor the other person's truth as well. To anyone I love, I promise to do the best I can to be honest, to share my feelings, to take responsibility for myself, to honor the connection I feel with that person, and to maintain that connection.

While we may have a strong desire and intention to maintain a certain form of relationship (a marriage for example), we can't have any absolute guarantees about a relationship's form. Real commitment allows for the fact that form is constantly changing, and that we can trust that process of change. It opens the door to the true intimacy that is created when people share deeply and honestly with each other. If two people stay together on this basis, it's because they really want to be together. They continue to find an intensity of love and learning with each other as they change and grow.

MONOGAMY OR NOT

People often ask me if I think monogamy is necessary in a primary relationship. I usually answer by sharing my own experience. As I mentioned earlier in this book, at one time in my life I experimented with nonmonogamous romantic relationships. I found that while I had wonderful ideals of love and freedom, emotionally it was way too painful for me. I also realized that one of my underlying motivations was my fear and ambivalence about commitment in relationship.

Once I learned about the many different selves within me, I realized that some of my inner selves are monogamous and some aren't! In fact, I found this to be fairly universal. We all have certain selves who would love to be free to relate sexually to others spontaneously, whenever they feel like it. We have other selves who need and desire the security and exclusivity of a monogamous relationship. The vulnerable child within us, in particular, will not really open up in a nonmonogamous relationship.

Since showing our deep vulnerability to another is a key to intimacy, if the vulnerable child is not present in a relationship, we will not experience the depth of closeness most of us yearn for in sexual partnership.

That level of intimacy is very important to me, so I came to the understanding that for me, a mutual commitment to monogamous behavior is an important element in my relationship with my partner. We understand that attractions to others are an inevitable part of being alive. We can feel and even enjoy those attractions while maintaining appropriate boundaries. If we are honest with ourselves and each other, these experiences can be part of our personal growth and the growth of our relationship.*

ROMANCE

When we meet someone who is a particularly strong mirror for us, we feel an intense attraction (or we may experience it initially as a repulsion or dislike; either way, there's a strong feeling). If that person is of the sex we prefer and has certain characteristics, we may experience the feeling as a sexual attraction. When the energy is particularly strong we have an experience we call "falling in love."

Falling in love is actually a powerful experience of feeling the universe move through you. The other person has become a channel for you, a catalyst that triggers you to open up to the love, beauty, and passion within you. Your own channel opens wide, the universal energy comes through, and you have a

---

* For more information on this issue, I recommend the book *Embracing Each Other* and the tapes *Affairs and Attractions* by Drs. Hal and Sidra Stone.

blissful moment of "enlightenment" very similar to the experiences some people have after long periods of meditation.

This is the most thrilling and passionate experience in the world and, of course, we want to hold on to it. Unfortunately, we don't realize that we are experiencing the universe within ourselves. We recognize that the other person has triggered this experience and we think it is him or her that is so wonderful! At the moment of falling in love, we are accurately perceiving the beauty of that person's spirit, but we may not recognize it as a mirror of our own. We just know that we feel this great feeling when we're with them. So, we often begin to give our power away to them, and start to put our source of happiness outside of ourselves.

The other person immediately becomes an object — something we want to possess and hold on to. The relationship becomes an addiction: as with a drug, we want more and more of the thing that gets us high. The problem is that we get addicted to the person's form, not recognizing that it's the energy we want. We focus on the personality and the body, and try to grab on to it, to keep it. The minute we do this, the energy gets blocked. By grabbing hold of the channel so tightly, we are actually strangling it and closing off the very energy we seek.

True passion brings us together, but our neediness often takes over shortly thereafter. The relationship starts to die almost as soon as it blooms. Then we really panic and usually hold on even tighter. The initial experience of falling in love was so powerful that we sometimes spend years trying to re-create it; but often, the more we try, the more it eludes us. It's only when we give up and let go that the energy may start to flow again and we can experience that same feeling.

Such is the tragic nature of romance in the old world. We've spent thousands of years trying to work this one out. Our favorite songs, stories, and dramas reflect and reinforce the externally addicted nature of our relationships and the resulting pain and frustration.

In the new world, we are discovering something simple and beautiful that can heal much of our pain: the greatest romance of all can be our love affair with life.

A LOVE AFFAIR

I am finding that being alive is a love affair with the universe. I also think of it as a love affair between my inner male and female, and between my form and my spirit.

As I build and open my channel, more and more energy flows through. I feel greater intensity of feeling and passion. Being in love is a state of being that is independent of any one person. Certain people, however, seem to intensify or deepen my experience of the life force within me. I know that those people are mirrors to me and that they are also channels for special energy in my life.

I move toward them because I want the intensification that I experience with them. I feel the universe moving through me to them, and moving through them to me. This could happen through any form of exchange. The energy itself lets me know what is needed and appropriate. It's a mutually satisfying and fulfilling exchange because the universe is giving each of us what we need. It may be a brief, one-time experience, a glance or a short conversation with a stranger. Or it may be an ongoing contact, a profound relationship that lasts for many years. I see it more and more as the universe coming to me constantly, through many different channels.

What I have just written is an ideal scene. I certainly am not living it fully at every moment. Many times I am caught up in my fears and insecurities. However, I am experiencing it more and more frequently, and when I do, it feels wonderful!

Exercises

1. Take yourself on a romantic date. Do everything as if you were going out with the most loving and exciting partner you can imagine. Take a luxurious hot bath, dress in your best clothes, buy yourself flowers, go to a lovely restaurant, take a moonlight stroll, do anything else that strikes your fancy. Spend the evening telling yourself how wonderful you are, how much you love yourself, and anything else that you would like to hear from a lover. Imagine that the universe is your lover and is giving you everything that you want.

2. The next time that you feel a romantic or a sexual "charge" with someone, remember that it's the universe you are feeling. Whatever you do, whether you act on it or not, just remember that it's all part of your true love affair with life.

Chapter Fifteen

OUR CHILDREN

*L*iving in connection with our intuition applies to parenting as much as to every other area of our lives. While I don't have children myself, I have a number of friends who are using these principles in relating to their children. It certainly isn't easy to transform our old concepts and patterns of raising children, but the results are wonderful to see: bright light radiating from these children, satisfaction and fulfillment for their parents, and the depth of closeness and sharing between them.

Our old ideas of parenting usually involve feeling totally responsible for the welfare of our children and trying to follow some behavior standard to be a "good parent." As you learn to trust yourself and be yourself spontaneously, you may find yourself violating many of your old rules about what a good parent does. Nevertheless, the energy and aliveness that are coming through you, your increasing sense of satisfaction in your life, and your trust in yourself and the universe will do far more to help your child than anything else possibly could.

In a sense, you don't have to "raise" your children at all! The universe is the true parent to your children; you are simply the channel. The more you are able to follow your energy and do what is best for you, the more the universe will come through you to everyone around you. As you thrive, your children will, too.

When babies are born, they are powerful, intuitive beings. Newly arrived in the physical world, they spend their first years learning to live in a body. Their *forms* are younger and less experienced than ours, but their *spirits* are just as developed as ours. In fact, I believe that we often have children who are spiritually more developed than we are, so that we can learn from them.

Our children come into the world as clear beings. They know who they are and what they are here to do. I believe that on some level of consciousness, parents and children have made an agreement. The parents have agreed to support and assist the child in developing his form (body, mind, and emotions) and learning how to operate in the world. The child has agreed to help the parents be more in touch with their intuitive selves. Because children have not yet lost their conscious connection to their spirit, they provide us with considerable support in reconnecting with our own higher selves.

Our children essentially need two things from us:

1. They need to be recognized for who they really are. If we see and know that they are powerful and sophisticated spiritual beings and relate to them that way from the beginning, they will not need to hide their power and lose touch with their soul, as many of us have. Their being will receive the support and acknowledgment they need to remain clear and strong.
2. They need us to create an example for them of how to live effectively in the world of form. As we do this, they watch how we live and imitate us. Being very perceptive and pragmatic, they copy what we actually *do*, and not what we *say*.

In return for taking responsibility for these two things, we receive from our children endless amounts of vibrant energy. Unless they are shut down at a very early age through lack of support, children are very clear and powerful channels. Because they have not yet developed much rational censorship, they are almost totally intuitive, completely spontaneous, and absolutely honest. From watching them, we can learn a great deal about how to follow energy and live creatively.

Most parents have not been able to fulfill their responsibilities as successfully as they would have wished. In general, parents have been confused about their roles and responsibilities. They haven't had any clear models or guidelines. Until very recently in human history, no one did much research on parenting, and there are still very few resources for educating oneself about how to be a parent. Most people parent in a rather hit-or-miss fashion. So everyone has made plenty of mistakes.

I've met a lot of parents who, now that they have become more conscious, feel tremendous guilt and sadness in looking back on how they've raised their children. It's helpful to remember that children are powerful, spiritual beings who are responsible for their own lives — they chose you as a parent so that they could learn the things they needed to work out in this lifetime.

Also, it helps tremendously to know that as you grow and evolve, they will be positively affected and supported by your transformation. They will change as you change, even if they are grown and live far away from you. All relationships are telepathic, so no matter what the physical distance, they will continue to reflect you.

Because we have not been sufficiently attuned to our own being, it's been hard to recognize and trust the spirit within our children. Because they were physically undeveloped and rationally unsophisticated, we thought they were less aware and less responsible than they really are.

I've observed in many people the underlying attitude that children are somewhat helpless or untrustworthy and that parents are responsible for controlling and molding them into responsible beings. Children, of course, pick up this attitude and reflect it in their behavior. If you recognize and treat them as powerful, spiritually mature, responsible beings, they will respond accordingly.

CHILDREN AS MIRRORS

Because young children are relatively unspoiled, they are our clearest mirrors. As intuitive beings, they are tuned in on a feeling level and respond honestly to the energy as they feel it. They haven't learned to cover up yet. When adults do not speak or behave according to what they are actually feeling, children pick up on the discrepancy immediately and react to it. Watching their reactions can help us become more aware of our own suppressed feelings.

For example, if you are trying to appear calm and collected when inside you are feeling upset and angry, your children may mirror this to you by becoming wild and disruptive. You are trying to maintain control, but they pick up on the chaotic energy inside of you and reflect it in their behavior. Oddly enough, if you express directly what you are truly feeling without trying to cover it up ("I'm feeling really upset and frustrated because I've had a rotten day. I'm mad at the world and at myself and at you! I want you to be quiet so I can have peace and quiet to try to sort out my feelings. Will you please go outside for a few minutes?"), they will usually calm down. They feel comfortable with the truth and the congruity between your feelings and your words.

Many parents think they have to protect their children from their (the parents') confusion or so-called negative feelings. They think that being a good parent means maintaining a certain role — always being patient, loving, wise, and strong. In fact, children need honesty — they need to see a model of a human being going through all the different feelings and moods that a human being goes through and being honest about it. This gives them permission and support to love themselves and allow themselves to be real and truthful.

Sharing your feelings with your children does not mean dumping your anger on them or blaming them for your troubles. It also does not mean you can expect them to be your partner or therapist and help you with your problems. The more you practice expressing your feelings honestly as you go along, the less likely you are to do these things. Being human, however, you probably will dump your anger or frustration on them from time to time. Once you see that you've done it, tell them you realize that you dumped on them and that you are truly sorry, and then let it go. It's all part of learning to be in close relationships.

Children also serve as our mirrors by imitating us from a very young age. We are their model for behavior, so they pattern themselves after us. Thus, we can watch them to see what we are doing! Children often reflect either our primary selves (in the ways they are similar to us) or our own disowned selves (in the ways they are different from us). When they behave in ways that we find upsetting or mystifying, they are usually acting out one or more of our disowned selves — our shadow side. For example, a woman friend of mine is a very sweet, loving person who is a committed pacifist. She was shocked and horrified to discover that her little boy loved playing with toy guns; of course, he was reflecting her disowned aggressive side!

When your child does something you don't like, tell him or her how you feel about it and deal with it directly, but also ask yourself in what way that behavior mirrors you or how you might be supporting it in your own process.

For example, if your children are being secretive and hiding things from you, ask yourself if you have been really open and honest about all your feelings with them. Is there something you are hiding from someone or from yourself? Is there some way you don't trust yourself and therefore don't trust them? If your children are being rebellious, take a look at the relationship between your own inner authoritarian and rebel. If your inner authoritarian has a lot of control in your life, your children may be acting out your suppressed rebellious side. Or, if you've acted out the rebel a lot in your life, they may be imitating you.

Take a good look at how these problems reflect your inner process. If you learn from your experiences and grow, so will your children. Externally, a lot of these problems can be worked through by deeply and sincerely sharing your feelings and learning to assert yourself, and by encouraging your children to do the same. You may want to get support from a professional counselor or family therapist to help the whole family change its old patterns.

I have found that, for many people, parenting has been a convenient excuse not to do their own learning and growing. Frequently, parents spend most of their time focusing on their children, trying to make sure that the children learn and grow properly. In taking responsibility for their children's lives, they abandon responsibility for their own lives. This has the unfortunate result of making the children feel, unconsciously, that they have to take responsibility for their parents (because their parents are sacrificing for them). Children may imitate their parents' behavior by taking responsibility for other people, or they may rebel against the pressure to conform to their parents' expectations by acting out the opposite of what their parents want.

Parents need to shift the focus of their responsibility from their children back to themselves, where it belongs. Remember that children learn by example. They will tend to do what you do, not what you tell them to do. The more you learn to take care of yourself and live a fulfilling, happy life, the more they will do the same.

This doesn't mean you should abandon or ignore your children. It doesn't mean that you let them do whatever they want. You are in a deep relationship with them and, like any other relationship, it takes a lot of caring and communication. It's important for all of you to express feelings, make needs known, and set clear boundaries. Furthermore, you have accepted certain responsibilities to care for them physically and financially. You have a right to require their co-responsibility and cooperation in that process.

The key is in your attitude. If you truly see your children as powerful, responsible entities and treat them as equal to you in spirit (while acknowledging that they are less experienced than you in form), they will mirror that attitude back to you.

From the time they are born, assume that they know who they are and what they want, and that they have valid feelings and opinions about everything. Even before they can talk, ask them for their feelings about things they are involved in and trust your intuition and the signals they give you to know what their answers are. For example, ask them if they'd like to be included in an outing or if they'd rather stay home with a babysitter. Trust your feelings about which choice they are making and proceed accordingly. Then pay attention to the signals they give. If you take them on an outing and they cry the whole time, next time try leaving them with the babysitter.

As they grow older, continue to include them in family decisions and responsibilities. As much as possible, allow them to make their own decisions about their personal lives.

This means they may sometimes have to deal with the consequences of making certain decisions. Offer them your love, support, and advice, but let it be understood that their lives are basically their own responsibility. Be sure you set your own boundaries clearly — what is okay and what isn't. Making their own decisions does not include the right to take advantage of you. Above all, try to communicate your honest feelings to them and ask them to let you know how they are feeling. Almost all family problems arise from lack of communication. Your children certainly aren't going to know how to communicate clearly if you don't know how.

It seems to be terribly difficult for parents to give up living their children's lives for them and start living their own. In order to do this, parents have to be willing to admit how dependent they really are on their children and how frightened they feel about letting go of them. These feelings are usually masked by a reverse projection — parents will tell themselves that their children are dependent on them and won't be okay if their parents start focusing on fulfilling their own needs.

I have found that this is a false issue. The real issue is the parents' feelings of dependency on their children, which they usually aren't even conscious of! Children are so alive and exciting, parents often secretly fear that their lives will be drab and dull without their children. Or perhaps they are just afraid to face themselves. Once they recognize and acknowledge these feelings, they will begin to deal with the emptiness within themselves and their lives. They will begin to look at what they want and how they can satisfy themselves. They will begin to trust their own gut feelings about things and act on them.

At this point, the children really start to flourish. They are finally liberated from the unconscious task of trying to take care of their parents; they are freed to make their own lives worthwhile! The children start doing what they really need to do for themselves. They can now become the channels they truly are.

One couple who are close friends of mine have a beautiful daughter. Since before she was born, her parents were aware of her as a powerful being and felt that they were in communication with that being. I was present at her home birth — a wonderful event. A few minutes after she was born, I was holding her and she looked strongly and directly into my eyes (I had previously heard that babies can't focus at such an early age). It was quite apparent to me that she was well aware of what was happening.

She has been raised much as I have described. She has always been afforded the respect that she deserves and has been treated as a highly conscious entity. As a result, she is a truly remarkable child. Wherever she goes, people remark on her strong presence. It's easy to see that she is an open channel for the universe.

Meditation

Get comfortable, relax, and close your eyes. Take a few deep breaths and move your awareness into a deep, quiet place within you.

Picture or imagine your child in front of you. Look into his or her eyes and sense the powerful being within. Take a little time just to be with this experience and receive any feelings, ideas, or impressions about who your child really is. Communicate to him or her, in your own words, your respect and appreciation. Imagine that your child is communicating to you his or her respect and appreciation.

If you have more than one child, do this with each one of them. This meditation is effective in opening the love and communication between you and your children, whether they are infants or adults.

Exercise

Practice telling the truth to your children and expressing your feelings honestly with them even if you feel vulnerable and uncomfortable about not being in control. Ask them how they feel about things and try to really listen to what they have to say. If you are tempted to give advice, first ask them if they want to hear it. If they don't, tell them your *feelings* instead.

Chapter Sixteen

WORK AND PLAY

*O*ur culture is obsessed with achievement and productivity. As a result we have an epidemic of workaholism in which most of us push ourselves much harder than is necessary or healthy. We need to learn to relax, nurture ourselves, and have fun. Some people carry the opposite polarity — they know how to relax and play but have difficulty focusing and working hard enough to accomplish things.

When you're following your energy and doing what feels right to you, moment by moment, the distinction between work and play tends to dissolve. Work is no longer what you *have* to do and play what you *want* to do. When you are doing what you love, you may work harder and produce more than ever before, but you will experience such enjoyment and pleasure in your work that at times it may feel like play.

Each one of us has a true purpose and each one of us is a unique channel for the universe. We make a contribution to the world just by being ourselves every moment. There need not be rigid categories in our lives — this is work, this is play. It all blends into the flow of following the universe, and money flows in as a result of the open channel that's created. Work is no longer something you have to do in order to survive and sustain life. You no longer work just for the sake of making money. Instead, the delight that comes from expressing yourself becomes the greatest reward. The money comes along as a natural part of being alive. For some, working and getting money may no longer even be directly related to each other; you may experience that you are doing whatever you have the energy to do and that money is coming into your life. It's no longer a matter of, "You do this and then you get money for it." The two things are simply operating simultaneously in your life but not necessarily in a direct cause-and-effect relationship.

In the new world, it's difficult to pin life's work and true purpose down to any one thing. In terms of looking for a career, our old world concept told us that when we became adults, we had to decide what our career would be and then pursue an education or other steps to achieve that career. The career would then be pursued for most, or all, of our life.

In the new world, many of us are channels for a number of things that may come together in fascinating combinations. Perhaps you haven't found your career because it doesn't exist yet. Your particular and unique way of expressing yourself has never existed before and will never be repeated again. As you practice following the energy in your life, it may lead you in many directions. You may express yourself in a variety of areas, all of which will begin to synthesize in some surprising, interesting, and very new creative ways. You will no longer be able to say, "I'm a writer (or a fireman or a teacher or a housewife)." You may be a combination of all of those things. You'll be doing what you love, what you're good at, what comes easily to you and has an element of challenge and excitement to it. Whatever you do will feel satisfying and fulfilling to you. It will no longer be a matter of doing things now for later gratification: "I will work hard now so that I can get a better job later. I will work hard now so that I can retire and enjoy my life. I will work hard now in order to have enough money and time to have a vacation where I can have fun." It's the fulfillment of what you're doing at this very moment that counts. When you are being a channel, everything you do becomes a contribution; even the simplest things are significant.

It is the energy of the universe moving through us that transforms, not just the specific things we do. When I write a book that has a certain impact on a reader's life, it's because of the energy of the universe that comes through me and connects to the reader's deeper levels of awareness. The words and ideas are the icing on the cake. They are the things that enable our minds to grasp what has already been changed. It is not so important that I wrote a book. What is important is that I expressed myself, opened up, and allowed the creative energy to flow through me. That creative energy is now penetrating other people and things in this world. I had the joy of that energy moving through me, and other people had the joy of receiving that energy. That's the transformational experience.

Whether you are washing the dishes, taking a walk, or building a house, if you're doing it with a sense of being right where you want to be and doing what you want to be doing, that fullness and joy in the experience will be felt by everyone around you. If you're building a house and people walk by and see you doing it, they will feel the impact of the fullness of your experience. Their lives will be transformed to the degree that they are ready to allow the energy's impact. Though they may not know what hit them, they will start to experience life differently. It's the same when you're just being. If you walk into a room feeling whole and expressing yourself in whatever way feels right to you, then everyone in the room will be affected and catalyzed in their own growth process. Even though they may not recognize it or know anything about it consciously, you may at times be able to see the direct result of your channel operating. You will see proof of it in watching the changes in people. It is an incredibly exciting and satisfying experience.

You can see that it may no longer be an issue of focusing on one lifelong career. At times in your life, you may be led to focus and build structure in one particular area of knowledge or expertise. You may choose to learn certain skills that you will use to allow your channel to function in a way that it wants to function. If you do this, you will be led through the learning experience easily and naturally. The process of learning will be just as satisfying as the doing. In other words, it is no longer necessary to sacrifice in the moment so that in the future you will be able to have what you want. The learning process can be fun, joyful, and exciting. You'll experience it as being exactly what you want to be doing at that time. Practicing, learning skills, going to school — all of this can be fun and fulfilling when you are following your intuitive guidance.

The work you do as a result will also be a learning experience. For example, I teach workshops, not because I've mastered the information and I am the expert, but because I love to share myself in this way. This sharing deepens my learning experience. Again, there is no strong boundary between learning and teaching, just as there is no wall between work and play. It all begins to blend and weave into one integrated and balanced experience.

Most people do have some sense, at least deep inside, of what they would love to be doing. This feeling is often so repressed, however, that it is experienced only in the form of some wildly impractical fantasy, something you could never do. I always encourage people to get in touch with these fantasies. Observe and explore thoroughly your most incredible fantasy of how you'd like to be and what you'd like to be doing. There is truth in this desire. Even if it seems impossible, there is at least a grain of truth in the image. It is telling you something about some part of you that's wanting to be expressed.

Your fantasies can tell you a great deal about yourself. Many times, I've found that people have a strong sense of what they would like to do, yet they take up a career that is very different from their desire. Sometimes they go for the opposite because they feel it is practical or will gain the approval of their parents or the world. They figure it is impossible to do what they really want, so they might as well settle for something else that comes along. I encourage people to risk exploring the things that really turn them on. The following are examples of people I've worked with and their exploration of their true purpose:

1. A brilliant and talented woman I know had been working with sick and dying people for many years. Although she was a great nurse and a powerful healer, it became evident to her that she needed to be where she could express herself more creatively. With encouragement, she started working fewer days as a nurse and began leading workshops and counseling people. Because she's doing this, she feels more fulfilled and those around her feel her fulfillment, as well.

2. Joseph was a young man in his early twenties. Following family tradition, he went into business with his father and brothers. He was very successful in real estate and contracting. The problem was, he knew there was something else he wanted to do with his life. After lots of encouragement from the group in one of my workshops, he admitted that he wanted to work in the arts but knew his family would frown on it. He most wanted to be a dancer. The first step was admitting to himself what he wanted to do. Eventually, he mustered the courage to take dance classes. He had a lot of talent and immediately attracted the attention of the teacher. He continued to explore this form of artistic expression. When he supported his desires, he actually found that his family was equally supportive.

3. A close friend of mine had three children and no college education and was living on welfare. Her desire was to get into business. She intuitively felt she was going to handle large amounts of money, but considering her situation, this didn't make sense. Nevertheless, she decided to explore some possibilities in the financial district of San Francisco. She was immediately hired as a receptionist; she went on to be an administrative assistant and continued to rise to higher levels of skill and responsibility. She eventually reached her goal of being a stockbroker. She loves what she's doing and her children are flourishing as well.

4. A woman who came to a recent workshop of mine shared that she'd been a talented pianist with hopes of becoming a concert pianist. Then, for several reasons, the most predominant being a lack of faith in herself, she had given up her dream. She started working in an office and found that between work and her children, she had little time for her music. After fifteen years, she felt it was simply too late to ever go back to the piano. She felt the time she had lost in not playing rendered hopeless any chance of being great. Despite all her doubts, we encouraged her to at least start playing again. I assured her that if she was doing what she loved, it would come back to her easily. As she opened to this idea, she started opening to herself. Her sense of hopelessness was replaced by a renewed sense of power. She called later to say she had been playing the piano and feeling great about it. A friend had asked her to play accompaniment for a choral group and she was feeling very excited about the musical possibilities starting to happen for her.

Meditation

Sit or lie down in a comfortable position. Close your eyes and relax. Take several slow, deep breaths, relaxing your body more deeply with each breath. Take several more breaths and relax your mind. Release and relax all the tension in your body. If you want, imagine that your body is almost sinking into the floor, bed, or chair.

From this very relaxed place inside, imagine that you are doing exactly what you want in your life. You have a fabulous career that is fun and fulfilling for you. You are now doing what you've always fantasized about and getting well paid for it.

You feel relaxed, energized, creative, and powerful. You are successful at what you do because it is exactly what you want to be doing.

You follow your intuition moment to moment and are richly rewarded for it.

Exercises

1. Follow any impulses you have in the direction of your true work/play/creative desires. Even if it seems totally unrealistic, follow the impulse anyway. For example, if you're sixty-five years old and have always wanted to be a ballet dancer, go to a ballet class and observe; or, if you want, take a beginning class. Watch some ballet and imagine that you're a dancer. While alone at home, put on

some music and dance. This will get you in touch
with the part of yourself that wants to be expressed
that way. You may end up dancing much more
than you thought possible, and you may be led to
other forms of expression that will feel as good.

2. List any fantasies you've had around work, career,
or creativity, and beside them, list the actions you
plan to take to explore them.

3. Write an "ideal scene" — a description of your
perfect job or career exactly as you would like
it to be. Write it in the present tense, as if it were
already true. Put in enough description and details
to make it seem very real. Put it away somewhere,
and look at it again in a few months or even a year
or two. Unless your fantasy has changed completely in that time, chances are that you will find
you have made significant progress in the direction
of your dream.

Chapter Seventeen

MONEY

*M*oney is a symbol of our creative energy. We have invented a system whereby we use pieces of paper or metal to represent a certain unit of creative energy. For example, you earn money by using your energy, then you trade that money to me in exchange for the energy I put into writing this book or leading a workshop, and so forth. Because the creative energy of the universe in all of us is limitless and readily available, so, potentially, is money. When we follow our inner guidance and move with the flow of energy in our lives, we find we have enough money to do the things we truly need and want to do. A shortage of money often mirrors the fact that our energy is blocked in other ways.

Your ability to earn and spend money abundantly and wisely is based on your ability to be a channel for the universe. The stronger and more open your channel is, the more will flow through it. The more you are willing to trust yourself and take the risks to follow your inner guidance, the more likely you are to have all the money you need. The universe will pay you to be yourself and do what you really love!

MONEY IN THE OLD WORLD

The old world is based on our attachment to the external, physical world. We look for satisfaction from external things. Because we believe that survival depends on getting things, we may think that fulfillment can be found in material wealth.

In the old world, you can build a strong financial structure and earn lots of money by learning how to act effectively in the world (the old male energy). However, because your actions are not based on the guidance of the universe that comes from the inner female, building your financial structure will often involve fear, competition, and struggle, and you will pay a high price for the money. You can earn money, but may find that you are ruled by it. You think the money itself is important: "If I have enough money, I can do these things and then I'll be happy," or "If I have enough money, then I'll feel good about myself and I'll be happy," or "Other people will like me if I have enough money and that will make me happy." From this point of view money is seen to be the important thing, but as long as it is valued in this way, money is always a problem.

If you have too little money, you're always struggling to get more money and always afraid there won't be enough. There's always that terrible pain inside that you don't have enough of what you need. On the other hand, from this perspective, even if you have a lot of money, it's painful because you're always afraid you're going to lose it. You can never have enough money to ensure that you won't be afraid.

People with little money seldom realize that people who have a lot of money are also frightened. They are basically insecure because they never know if they might lose their money. Circumstances out of their control might arise — they might make a foolish investment or somebody might steal their money. If security is based on having money, it doesn't matter whether you have a little or a lot, you're going to be afraid.

If we don't realize that money is a symbol of infinite energy, and we think there is only a limited amount of it in the world, we're stuck with two options: we can choose to have a lot of money and feel guilty, or we can choose to do without and resent those who have more. If you choose to have money, you will live with the knowledge that others have less than you. You may fear that your having more causes others to have less. You may choose to deal with the guilt by trying to deny or ignore the feeling, or you may choose to ease your conscience by attempting to help those who are less fortunate.

On the other hand, you can choose to say, "I won't carry that guilt. I won't take more than my share. I don't care about money anyway. Therefore, I will keep what I have to a minimum. I'll make sure that I am not taking from somebody else." The problem with this attitude is that you may end up feeling deprived. You see all the beautiful, wonderful things in the world that you would like to have and enjoy, but you can't. You see other people who have more than their share of money and you resent them. Basically, in this old world framework, we must choose either guilt or resentment.

The old world structure demands we do things out of our individual strength, instead of allowing the universe to do it. We think we have to work really hard to get what we want — the work ethic that says, "Work hard. Sacrifice and struggle." Most of us have that so deeply embedded in us that we don't allow ourselves to succeed financially or in any other way except through hard work, struggle, and sacrifice. If you are succeeding and making money, you are also paying a price emotionally, and often physically. People frequently drive themselves to the point of sickness or death. They struggle and sacrifice emotionally, and in the end, even though they have achieved worldly success, they still feel deprived and empty.

Or people refuse to go after it at all. "Look what it leads to: struggle, sacrifice, pain, and deprivation of oneself, so I simply won't deal with it. I'll get by on the absolute minimum amount of money in my own life." Often, more sensitive, spiritually inclined people choose this route so they can focus on more "meaningful" things. The problem with this is you're actually depriving yourself of dealing with one of the most exciting and beautiful things in life. If you're denying money, you're also denying a big part of the energy of the universe and the way the world works. People who choose the denial route usually don't know how to handle money and refuse to learn anything about it.

MONEY IN THE NEW WORLD

The new world is based on trust of the universe within us. We recognize that the creative intelligence and energy of the universe is the fundamental source of everything. Once we connect with this and surrender to it, everything is ours. Emptiness is filled from the inside.

We realize that money is a reflection of the energy moving through our channel. *The more we learn to operate in the world based on trust in our intuition, the stronger our channel will be and the more money we are likely to have.* The money in our life is based on our ability to listen to our inner guidance and risk acting on it. When you let go of trying to control and you learn how to listen to the universe and act on it, money increasingly comes into your life. It flows in an easy, effortless, and joyful way because there is no sacrifice involved. You're no longer attached to it. Instead, you can experience the joy of learning how to follow the energy of the universe. Money is an extra bonus in the process.

You know that the money is not really yours — it belongs to the universe. You act as a caretaker or steward for the money. You use it only as you are directed by the universe through your own intuition. There is no fear of loss because you know you are always taken care of. The money may come or go, but you can't lose the joy and fulfillment in your life. When you feel this secure and free, you often attract more and more money, so that you are continually pushed to deepen your trust at more intense levels with higher stakes. Ultimately, as channels, many of us will be called upon to handle large amounts of money from this place of surrender and commitment to the higher power. This is one of the ways that the power of the universe can be wielded effectively to transform the world.

ACTIVE AND RECEPTIVE

There are active and receptive aspects of the process of channeling money, as in every other creative process. The masculine, or active, way of making money is to go after something. You see something you want and go for it. The feminine, or receptive, way of making money is to attract what you want to you.

We have to be able to do both. We need to release the outgoing energy that wants to move toward a certain goal and risk fearlessly acting on it. We also need to practice nurturing ourselves, appreciating ourselves, and becoming attuned to our inner selves so that we can attract and receive what we want. Many people are developed on one side or the other. Either they know how to go after things but have a hard time attracting things to them, or they know how to attract things but are afraid to go after them. Often a balancing process is necessary. You may need to learn to receive the gifts, appreciation, love, and energy coming to you. Or you may need to practice outflowing your energy into the world, which keeps it flowing through your channel. This way, the energy doesn't get blocked on either end.

This means, on a practical level, you have to be willing to take some risks in the area of work and money. If you do only what you think you *should* do in order to make money and be secure, then you won't listen to the intuitive voice that tells you what you really *need* to do.

This can be very scary when it entails your job and your money. People often want to know, "What do I do if my intuition tells me not to go to work one day? What do I do then? Will I lose my job?" If taking off a day from work seems too risky, it may not be the best choice for you yet. You may need to strengthen your channel by following your impulses in smaller ways at first. You may call in and take half a day off or you may plan for a three-day weekend. One day, though, you may wake up and know, "I just don't want to go to work," and you will follow through with this and feel good about it. Usually, when my insides tell me to take time off, I need some nurturing, some peace and quiet, some creative time for inspiration to come through, or time to simply feel old feelings stirring up inside, feelings that need to be felt and released.

If you risk following your impulse, you'll find, maybe a few hours or days later, your energy will actually be renewed. You'll be able to go back and do what needs to be done in a fourth of the time. You'll do it in a much more inspired and creative way. Anything can happen if you risk and trust yourself. While home, you may receive a phone call from a person offering you a better job that pays much more money (that happened to a friend of mine). You may get a creative inspiration that will open up a fun, prosperous opportunity for you, or you may get an inspiration to go visit someone who will give you a lead to a great adventure. If you hate your job, though, your energy for it won't come back. Also, because your true creative energy is blocked, you'll continue to feel blocked financially. Eventually, you will probably leave your job because you cannot stay stuck in such a place for long.

Basically, the whole issue of money is doing what you really want to do as much of the time as possible. The universe will reward you for taking risks on its behalf. It's important, though, that the risks you take are proportionate to the level of structure you're building. In other words, if you're just beginning to learn how to trust and follow your intuition, you probably don't want to make a million-dollar deal on a gut feeling. You probably don't want to leap off a building and hope that you can fly. It is important that you build small things first. Practice following your intuition in everyday things. Say no, even though you're feeling pressured to say yes. Do the thing you want to do even though you don't know why. Do it on an impulse. Make that call. Enroll in that class. Think of the things you love to do, and do them. This will strengthen you to the point where you can make the big leaps.

BALANCE

Once you understand the basic process of learning how to follow your intuition and act on it, you have your groundwork for channeling money. There are, though, some aspects of relating more specifically to money that are important to know.

Balance is an important quality to develop in building the structure of your channel. If you have been extreme in one direction, you may have to go to the extreme in the other direction in order to integrate and balance both aspects of everything. For example, if you have been very careless and casual about money, or if you have been a person who has denied the existence or importance of money in your life, you may need to build structures specifically related to money. These include learning to balance your checkbook, budgeting money, and gaining an understanding of the rules that govern how money works in the world. You will find these practices interesting, even fascinating. They are no longer something that will block you from the spirit; they will open the way for you to have more spirit flowing through you.

People who have little understanding of money have usually chosen to avoid structure on one level or another because they feel rules, regulations, and details will keep them from experiencing the magic of life. They're afraid they'll spend all their time in their rational mind, instead of following their flow. If you have this fear, tune in and ask the universe for guidance. You'll want to do this in a way that makes you feel good. Perhaps it would help to hire someone to show you how to organize your finances. It does not have to be a painful process. You'll find it to be energizing and supportive in your life, as opposed to painful and boring.

Those who have already applied a great deal of structure to working with money in the world may need to let go and relax that structure. It's time to stop following your rules and allow the inspired aspect of the spirit of money to work in your life. Trust your intuition to guide you, and take more risks in doing things differently than usual.

Similarly, if you've been a person who has saved your money and been very careful about spending it, you need to learn to spend more impulsively based on your intuition.

Spend on the basis of a gut feeling of wanting something. Learn to follow these impulses and you'll find you won't end up broke. In fact, it actually creates a greater flow of money in your life. You're able to release and give it out, based on your intuition.

If you have been a spendthrift and always spent more than you actually have, you will probably need to plan more and budget. Again, do it in accordance with an inner feeling. If you're open to it, your intuition will tell you, "Hey, learn something about planning. Learn something about budgeting." It will support and help you. It won't make you feel restricted. If you follow your intuition about this, you will be led to people who can show you how to do it, and it will be an interesting process. Again, it will support your channel.*

FOCUS

Another important thing to know about how money works is that it will always flow into whatever you've created in your life to receive it. Because it's energy, it will be attracted to what you need or want or envision. If you have always operated on a survival level with money, having only enough money to take care of your basic needs, that's where your money will go. If you start to attract more money into your life, you may have the tendency to increase your basic needs and still only make enough to survive.

---

* If you have serious chronic money problems or debts, I recommend getting help from Debtors Anonymous, one of the 12-step programs.

That's what happened to me for a long time. I had an under-lying program that said, "I can only have as much money as I
need. It's not okay to have more than I need." Consequently, I
created more needs, and ones that weren't particularly rewarding. My car would break down and I'd have expensive repair
bills, or my cat would get sick and I'd have an expensive vet bill.
Any extra money that came in would go toward something that
was an emergency or a basic need. There was still nothing extra
for fun and creative play or greater luxury.

I found that I needed to create a budget that included
what I wanted as well as what I needed. I started at a reasonable level: "I'd like to buy at least one item of clothing each
month that's fun or more luxurious. I'd also like to do some
activity that would be fun." I would include these in my budget and the money for them would then flow in. That's the
power of budgeting. A budget is like a blueprint. If you create
a list, a picture in your mind of what you want to have in your
life, you will create the necessary money. You can just keep
expanding step by step.

MY MONEY HISTORY

For most of my adult life I had very little money. I never
focused much on money; I wasn't particularly interested in it.
Essentially, I did whatever I had to do to pay my rent and bills,
but I put most of my time and attention into my education and
my pursuit of consciousness and creative expansion.

I always did whatever I needed to get the money — various projects, housework, odd jobs, even my own business.

Only one time in my entire life did I have a nine-to-five job —
for six months!

I was used to living on the edge without much sense of
where my money was coming from. In those years, I learned
to trust that somehow the money would be there. Sometimes I
would get down to my last dollar and then, somehow or other,
more money would come. I was always cared for.

Then, gradually, as I began to use this process more and
more, learning to trust my intuition and act on it, learning to
listen to my inner guidance and risk putting myself out in the
world, I developed a career counseling people, teaching workshops, writing, and publishing books. As I followed my passion, I began to earn more money and to lead a more abundant
lifestyle. It continued to the point where I was actually making a good income and living in a beautiful apartment, doing
most of the things that I wanted to do. I came to count on that
amount of money, although it was never a secure thing. I was
still living from month to month, but money always seemed to
keep flowing. I constantly affirmed my trust in the universe to
take care of me, and I tried to follow its guidance.

But a time came, all of a sudden, when I had no money.
Some unexpected things happened and I was caught short.
I paid my rent and my bills, and I looked in my checkbook
and there was nothing left. I didn't have any savings or other
resources to fall back on. That was a very startling experience
because by that time, I was used to having a certain amount of
money.

What amazes me about this experience is that I had only
five minutes of fear. I thought, "Oh my god, what am I going
to do?" Then I felt totally calm. I had to have that five minutes

of fear — and then it was as if there were no more fears about money left after that. I knew I was going to be okay.

A key point to this is that I knew I would be willing to do whatever the universe asked me to do. I remember thinking, "Well, I love my apartment, but I could give it up. I love all the things I have, but I could give them up. If the universe wants me to go live in a tent in someone's backyard, I'll do that. It will probably be wonderful."

There was an incredible feeling of trust and knowing that none of the things I might lose were that important. Whatever I did next, even though it might be totally different, would be wonderful, too. I would be taken care of. It wasn't just an intellectual knowing, because I had already known this *intellectually* for a long time. Living through those five minutes of fear left me with a feeling of fearlessness. Emotionally, I knew that I was okay. It was a very profound experience.

I ended up cutting back a little bit on my expenses and lifestyle. That felt fine and I didn't feel deprived at all. In fact, it was a nice discipline for a while. Everything I needed was provided. Money came in to cover my expenses and I had a feeling of relief. I knew I had come to the level of income my form could currently handle. I wasn't ahead of myself in any way, and from then on, it was as if I came to earth and was building from a solid foundation. At that moment, I felt I was standing on a strong base of trust in the universe. From then on, I knew the amount of money in my life would keep expanding, and I would never go back to not having.

After that happened, there was an increasing flow of money in my life. I moved to a new level of business and finance that I had never dealt with before. I had become really good at learning how to follow the universe on one level, but the new challenge was learning to trust at a more expanded level where the stakes were higher.

In confronting this new level of prosperity, I felt at first rather ignorant and helpless. I knew I needed help, so I asked the universe to send me the right people to teach and guide me in this area. After interviewing a number of different financial advisers, I was led to both an accountant and a business manager who were perfect for me and who helped me learn what I needed to know.

Like most people, I have found that as my income expands, my expenses and responsibilities seem to expand right along with it! Interestingly enough, it seems to work in reverse as well; I always seem to create exactly as much money as I need to support the lifestyle I have created. Sometimes, when I'm confronted with a large, unexpected expense, I wonder how it's going to get handled. One way or another, it always does, often in surprising and unexpected ways.

It frequently seems as if some higher power within me is watching over me and making the whole thing work. My job is to keep learning more on a practical level about managing my business and financial situation while continuing to do my inner work of learning not to push myself so hard, and how to relax and receive more easily. The more I bring myself into balance, the more smoothly money flows in my life.*

Here is a wonderful story that illustrates the miraculous way the universe works when we trust and follow our intuition.

---

* For more of my ideas and practical techniques about money and prosperity, please read *Creating True Prosperity*.

In the original edition of *Living in the Light*, I wrote about
buying a piece of property in Hawaii because I had a strong
intuitive feeling that it was the right thing to do. Logically,
it did not make sense, and my financial advisers were not in
favor of it. Still, I went ahead because it felt right to me. One
factor in this decision was the fact that this beautiful land was
about to be bought by an unscrupulous and exploitative devel-
oper. At the time I wrote the book, I wasn't quite sure what
would happen next, but I felt very empowered by trusting
myself that much.

Subsequently, I had many moments of doubting that decision. I wanted to create a home and a retreat center in Hawaii,
but I soon realized this piece of land was not large enough.
Also, this land was on Maui and I felt strongly that I needed
to be on Kauai. I eventually decided to sell this property. It
took quite some time before it was sold, however, and ultimately the transaction resulted in a moderate financial loss
for me. Since the sale was handled by an agent, I didn't meet
the purchasers of the property. I chalked the whole thing up
to a learning experience and eventually bought the property I
really wanted on Kauai.

A few years later, my mother, who lives on Maui, happened to meet the two men who had bought my property.
They told her this amazing story:

They had been living in Los Angeles, working hard and
longing for a big change in their lives. They read my book
Creative Visualization and decided to move to Hawaii. They
began visualizing the ideal property they would like to find
there, and got a very vivid image and feeling about it.

They took a trip to Maui and looked at many pieces of

property, but none was right. Just as they were about to leave, they went to see one last piece, and it was exactly as they imagined! Someone else had put in an offer, but that offer fell through, and they were able to buy it. Only when they signed the papers did they realize that they were buying my property!

We eventually became friends. They developed the property beautifully, creating a lovely flower farm and bed and breakfast, and have lived there happily for many years. I now feel that I was guided to buy that property in order to make sure that it got to the people who were meant to care for it. I may have lost some money, but I gained enormous satisfaction.

Meditation

Sit or lie down in a position that is comfortable for you. Close your eyes and begin breathing in an easy, natural way. With each breath, you are becoming more deeply relaxed.

Begin to notice how you're feeling. How do you feel emotionally? How does your body feel? Notice the energy in your body. What does it feel like? See yourself taking in more energy with each breath. You are energized and alive.

Start to imagine this energy as money. As you open to your own energy, you open to abundance.

Imagine having all the money you need to do the things that are most important to you, and to create a lifestyle that is in harmony with your being and with the earth.

Exercise

Lack of money may mirror the energy blocks within you. Write down all the ways in which you limit your desires and creativity. In what ways are you not doing what you want to do?

Some examples of this:

1. I'm doing administrative work in an office when I'd rather be working with children.
2. I want to meditate, but there's never time.
3. I'd like to explore my art more, but I have no time; I have to earn a living.
4. I want to tell my mother (friend, partner) how I'm feeling, but am afraid I'll hurt her (him).

Now imagine yourself doing exactly what you want to do in each of these areas.

Chapter Eighteen

HEALTH

Our body is our primary creation, the vehicle we have chosen to express us in the physical world. By looking at our bodies, listening to them, and feeling them, we can read a great deal about our spiritual, mental, and emotional energy patterns. The body is our primary feedback mechanism that can show us what is and isn't working about our way of thinking, expressing, and living.

Any normal child, who has had a reasonably positive environment, has a beautiful, lively body filled with vitality. That beauty, aliveness, and vitality are simply the natural energy of the universe flowing freely through, unimpeded by negative habits. Small children in a supportive environment are totally spontaneous beings. They eat when they are hungry, fall asleep when they are tired, and express exactly what they feel. Therefore, their energy doesn't get blocked, and they are constantly renewed and revitalized by their own natural energy.

But because none of us have had even a close-to-perfect upbringing, very early we begin to develop habits that run counter to our natural energy. These habits are designed to help us survive in the neurotic world in which we find ourselves. We pick these patterns up from our families, friends, teachers, and the community in general.

As we follow the behavior we have observed in others, or as we attempt to follow the rules laid down by others, we may move in ways that are counter to our own natural flow. We stop acting on what we know physically and emotionally; we no longer say and do what we really feel. We stop listening to the signals our body gives us about the food, rest, exercise, and nurturing it needs. It becomes too risky to follow our own energy, so we block that flow and gradually begin to experience less and less energy and vitality. As the energy flow diminishes, the body is not physically revitalized as quickly; thus, it begins to age and deteriorate. As we repeat chronic negative behaviors, our bodies begin to reflect these patterns, such as hunching over to express the inner pattern of making oneself small and powerless.

If you are willing to allow the energy of the universe to move through you by trusting and following your intuition, you will increase your sense of aliveness and your body will reflect this with increasing health, beauty, and vitality. Every time you don't trust yourself and don't follow your inner truth, you decrease your aliveness and your body will reflect this with a loss of vitality, numbness, pain, and eventually physical disease.

Dis-ease is a message from our bodies, telling us that, in some way, we are not following our true energy or supporting our feelings. The body gives us many such signals, starting with relatively subtle feelings of tiredness and discomfort. If we don't pay attention to these cues and make the appropriate changes, our bodies will give us stronger signals, including aches, pains, and minor illnesses. If we still don't change, a serious or fatal illness or accident may eventually occur. The stronger messages can often be avoided by paying attention to the subtler ones. But once a strong message has come, it is never too late to be healed, if that is what we truly desire. At this point, however, many beings do not choose the healing. They decide to leave their bodies and start over with a new one (or move to another realm) rather than trying to work their way through all the old patterns in this one.

If you are suffering from dis-ease, rest. Your body always wants rest and ease if it's sick. Then, when you've become quiet, ask your body what the message in your illness is. Your body will always attempt to tell you what you need in order to heal yourself.

One of my friends had been having severe pain on the right side of her face. Intuitively, she felt the pain would ease if she'd open her mouth and state more of what she wanted and more of what she knew. She did this and the pain eased some, but it still wasn't gone. One night, in a mood of surrender, she told the universe she was sick of the whole thing and she asked for an answer. Then she let go of thinking about the problem and went to sleep. In her dreams that night, her intuition told her to stop taking brewer's yeast. At first she discounted the entire message as bizarre and continued to take yeast. Then a few days later, after continued prodding from her intuition, she stopped taking yeast. Two days later, her face pain cleared up.

When you ask for a healing, you never know what your body is going to tell you. It may tell you to stop or start eating something, express some feelings to a friend, quit your job, or go see a doctor. The key is to ask and then listen for a response.

A client came to me who had been suffering from severe back pain for a year and a half. During the session, I asked him to contact the pain and ask his body what it was trying to tell him. In doing this, he realized he had not yet grieved his mother's death or expressed the anger he felt toward his father. He was holding both anger and sadness in his back. Recognizing this relieved some of the pain. After more talking, he was able to cry about his mother's death. Shortly after this, he became willing to express his anger toward his father. He started by talking to me about it, as well as writing out all his feelings. His back pain went away. His back pain has continued to be a barometer of suppressed feelings: he knows now that if he's in pain he needs to "back himself up" by expressing some feelings.

Once we've developed a symptom, it can recur if the behavior recurs. Our bodies serve us by accurately informing us of any blocked energy. Below I've listed some common causes of pain or illness in the body. These may or may not be accurate for you. Each is accompanied by a healing affirmation, in italics. Use them if they feel right for you, or make up your own.

Headache: two conflicting energies or feelings within; allow both sides to have a voice.

I am now willing to hear all my feelings.

Cold: the body needs rest, a clearing out of the old; the body needs to get back into balance.

I am now willing to let go of the old. I now have rest and ease in my life. My body is in perfect harmony.

Complexion problems: held back male energy; a need to take action and/or express yourself more directly.

I go all out for what I feel and what I want. I express my feelings clearly and directly.

Skin rashes: wanting to break out and take action; ask yourself, "What am I itching to do?"

I act on what my intuition tells me. I am willing to try new things. I do what I want to do.

Allergies: a lack of trust in the intuitive or instinctual energies; repressed feelings; allergies related to watery eyes are often indicative of suppressed sadness.

I trust and express my feelings. It's safe to feel and express my sadness and anger.

Back pain: a feeling that you have to support others, the world. A need to express and support your feelings; lower back pain is often suppressed sadness; upper back pain is often suppressed anger.

I support all my feelings. I take care of myself. I express and trust my feelings. I trust others to take proper care of themselves.

Menstrual cramps: not fully listening to and honoring your female aspect; a need to be quiet and go within.

I honor my female completely and act on what she tells me to do. I relax, rest, and nurture myself regularly.

Vision problems: not wanting to look at certain things within yourself or in the world. Often there is a decision early in life not to look at what you are intuitively "seeing" because it is too painful; when the inner vision is shut down, the external vision is impaired as well.

I am now willing to see everything in my life clearly.

Hearing problems: needing to shut out external voices and influences; needing to listen more to your inner voice.

I don't have to listen to anyone else. I listen to, and trust, my own inner voice.

ADDICTION

The more uncomfortable we are about trusting our natural energy, the more likely we are to use drugs such as coffee, cigarettes, alcohol, unwholesome foods or too much food, marijuana, speed, cocaine, or whatever, to attempt to manipulate our energy. We thereby deplete and denigrate the body further.

Most people are afraid of their energy and power. They're afraid of being either too much or too little; they're afraid of having too much energy or not enough. The truth is, if people would be willing to let go of using addictive substances, they'd find their own perfect flow of energy. By doing this, they'd tap their true source of power and creativity.

I see addiction as a means people use to pace (control) this power. Many powerful and creative people become addicts because they do not have an internal strength to support their energy. Without a trust in the universe, one's power and creativity can seem overwhelming. With substances, you can force your natural energy or you can dampen it, but either way, you're stopping the natural flow of the universe coming through.

You don't have to be a full-blown addict to realize you're using a substance to manipulate your energy. You may realize you're drinking three cups of coffee to energize yourself, only to feel depleted later. (We are a nation addicted to coffee, which I consider a strong drug because it seriously impairs your ability to trust and follow your energy.)

The key is to notice what you're doing. Become aware of when and why you use coffee. Notice how it changes your energy. Eventually, you will find that you don't need to pay that price anymore.

Realize that we all use some form of addiction to pace ourselves. The cure for this is to build trust in ourselves and the universe. Become increasingly willing to experience your own power and strength. This is the true healing.

For those who have a drug or alcohol addiction, noticing that you're pacing yourself is not enough. It may make you more aware of your problem and how shut down you are, but generally the physical craving overwhelms any awareness. Because of this, I encourage people to get help and support through a group such as Alcoholics Anonymous or Narcotics Anonymous to recover from alcohol or drug addiction. This gives the body a chance to heal and the spirit and emotions a chance to be heard.

For more information about self-healing, you may wish to read my book *The Four Levels of Healing: A Guide to Balancing the Spiritual, Mental, Emotional, and Physical Aspects of Life.*

Meditation

Sit or lie down, close your eyes, and take a few deep breaths. With each breath, feel your body letting go into a deeply relaxed place. Relax your mind and let your thoughts drift. Try not to attach yourself to any thoughts you're having. Feel yourself relax into a quiet place within.

This deep place is a source of nourishment and healing for you. Know that you can go here and find anything you need to know to heal yourself. If you've been having a problem with your health or you have a question you want to ask your intuition about your body, take the opportunity to do this now.

Ask, "What do I need to do to heal myself now? What does my body need?" When you've asked, stay open to any answers that will come to you. An answer or an intuitive feeling may come right away, or it may come in the next couple of days. It may come to you in a direct solution or you may be guided to a person or place that will give you the answers you need.

Know that you can heal yourself and that limitless wisdom lies within you.

Say these affirmations silently or aloud: "I am now healing myself. I am energized, alive, and filled with radiant health."

Alternative Meditation

If there is a particular part of your body that is sick or in pain, try this meditation. Get comfortable, take a few deep breaths, completely relax your body and mind. Now put your consciousness into that place and ask it what it is feeling and what it is trying to tell you. Then be receptive to feeling and hearing what its message to you is. Ask that part of your body what you need to do to heal yourself. Pay attention to, and follow, whatever it tells you.

Chapter Nineteen

YOUR PERFECT BODY

*H*aving a beautiful body starts with following the natural flow of your energy. Trust yourself. Express yourself physically in ways that feel good. Sleep as much as you need to. Stay in bed if you feel you need more rest. Eat what your body truly desires and follow your heart. If you're willing to trust your body, you'll learn what's best for you.

It sounds simple enough. The problem is that we've been taught to distrust our bodies and see them as needing to be controlled. Some religions even suggest that the spirit is good and the body is a weak, sinful tool of the devil. Although we have evolved to the point where these beliefs are not generally expressed openly, we still respond to our bodies with mistrust. As a culture, we're accustomed to ignoring our bodies and their needs. Our minds tell our bodies what to do. We decide that a nine-to-five workday, with three meals a day, is a "reasonable" way to live; then we expect our bodies to cooperate, even if this doesn't feel good. We've also developed, intellectually, theories for what's good for us and what isn't, what foods we should and shouldn't eat.

As children, we usually adopt parental and societal rules and habits regarding food. Even if you want to eat something else for dinner or want to eat at a different time, you're most likely expected to conform to the norms of the system. The body can tell you one thing and society another. Many of us learn to distrust ourselves at an early age. This distrust causes internal conflict and an imbalance in our system. It can set up a lifelong battle between the authoritarian and rebel voices within us. When we rebel, we may find ourselves craving all kinds of things we would not normally desire if left to our natural flow. We may develop the habit of going for the quickest available high. Our bodies may react to this imbalance by gaining weight, becoming hyperkinetic, losing weight, or developing food addictions and allergies. Then, to solve these problems, we may try even harder to control ourselves by following a rigid, restrictive diet. This causes us to feel deprived, so eventually the rebel takes over again and brings on the very foods we were trying to avoid.

We may play out this same conflict in regard to physical exercise. Many people believe the only way they can keep their bodies in shape is to push themselves to exercise in a very driven way. We may resist this by becoming lethargic and never exercising at all.

Our society fosters this struggle and profits from it. We are constantly shown what a beautiful body should look like, and are sold ways of getting there. We are sold diets, miracle weight-loss plans, low-calorie or fat-free foods, and health club memberships. We are constantly beating our bodies into some new idea of health and beauty. The problem with the external pictures and "shoulds" we adapt from outside of ourselves is that we are constantly dissatisfied with the way we look or the way we feel.

The way to a healthy, strong, and beautiful body is to learn to trust and love yourself. You can begin this process by becoming aware of all the rules and ideas you have about how you should look and feel, what you should eat, how you should exercise, and so on. It can help to write these down, adding more to the list whenever you become aware of another belief or rule. The process of writing down these ideas can help you become less identified with them, so that you can begin to have more choice about which ones, if any, you want to follow. In the process of doing this, you may discover more of your inner primary selves, such as the perfectionist (who has very high ideals it wants you to live up to), the pusher (who drives you to accomplish the perfectionist's goals), and the critic (who constantly reminds you of how you are failing).

Once you gain some awareness of these ideas and energies, and are not so unconsciously controlled by them, you can begin to ask yourself what you truly want and tune into your own intuitive feelings about what is really right for you.

Your own body and your intuition are, ultimately, the best guides about what is good for you and how to take care of yourself. You may find that once you are paying attention, your body will spontaneously let you know what it needs to eat and how it wants to move and exercise. Some people find that just by following their energy, they develop their own personal diet and exercise program that is exactly what their body needs, and this may change from time to time. For example, at certain times, their body may want to exercise vigorously, in which case it feels wonderfully exhilarating and satisfying. At other times, it may want to rest or exercise very gently.

Many people find that they need additional information and structure, in which case their inner guidance leads them to the appropriate books, nutritionist, exercise coach, doctor, or teacher. It is perfectly fine and can be very helpful to follow someone else's diet or exercise program as long as it feels right for you.

The process of healing your relationship to your body may take some time and require some help and support. Our feelings about our bodies are usually connected to very deep issues related to our self-esteem, our identities, our families, our sexuality, and so on. It can be helpful to have the support of a therapist while exploring these core issues.

If you have chronic weight problems, food addictions, or an eating disorder and are not currently in therapy, I strongly recommend seeking help from a therapist, support group, or treatment program that specializes in these issues. Fortunately these days, there are many excellent programs and counselors in this field. Many people also find help in this area through Overeaters Anonymous, one of the 12-step programs, which are free and available in most cities.

ASSERTION

One of the most important keys to creating a healthy, beautiful body is learning to assert yourself consistently in your life. I have found that many people with body issues have a pattern of doubting themselves, of being afraid to trust their feelings and act on them. They especially need to learn how to say no to others when they don't want to do something. Many overweight people I've worked with don't have strong personal boundaries; they try to please and take care of others and allow others to intrude on them and take advantage of them. Thus, they need to use extra weight as a buffer, a way of creating some distance from others.

Women, in particular, may fear that by becoming slim, they will be too sexually attractive. They are afraid of attracting unwanted attention or energy, and don't trust themselves to know how to deal with it. Some people are afraid of feeling too sensitive and vulnerable and not knowing how to protect themselves. Others are afraid of being too "spaced out"; they use their weight to ground them. If you have these fears, you can diet forever and you will not lose weight or keep it off because you are unconsciously needing it.

This is why the process of assertion is so vital. When you learn to back up your feelings with action, you create an internal strength and protection. You feel safe to move into new situations and attract attention and energy, knowing that you will be able to say no to anything that doesn't feel good to you. You know that you will be true to yourself and take good care of yourself. Your female aspect feels safe and supported, knowing that your inner male will back her up.

My experience has been that once people learn assertion, they are able to lose weight more easily and naturally without deprivation. The increased energy circulation in their bodies dissolves the blocked energy, and the extra weight gradually melts away. They no longer need it for strength or protection, so they release it effortlessly. If any particular diet is needed, they are guided to the appropriate nutritionist or diet plan; or they feel intuitively what they need to be eating, and find it appropriate and enjoyable to do so.

WAITING = EXCESS WEIGHT

If you're always waiting to be, do, or have what you want, your energy gets blocked and your body may reflect this in excess weight. When you express yourself directly and do what you want when you want (asserting yourself), energy will move freely through your body, and this circulation will dissolve excess weight. The more you're willing to be yourself, the less you'll need to use food as a substitute nurturer; you'll be receiving the natural nurturing of the universe.

The key to self-assertion is to take action on your feelings and intuition. I've seen people lose weight simply by doing something they've been afraid to do or by expressing some feeling they've suppressed. By continuing to do this, you dissolve blocks and your weight balances out.

At first, the prospect of asserting yourself moment to moment can be frightening. We're not used to stating what we need and taking action to give it to ourselves. It takes a conscious effort to tune into how we feel and risk taking action. Once you start doing this, though, it feels so good that you'll want to keep doing it. You'll lose weight, have more energy, and look more alive and beautiful. There really is no turning back. The alternative is numbness and death. Every time I follow my inner voice, I feel more life energy flowing through me. Every time I go against it, I can feel a struggle in my body, and a heaviness and tiredness. If I continue to push myself past what my body wants, I become increasingly tired and lifeless.

One of my clients was about eighty pounds overweight when she started working with me. She tried every conceivable weight-loss program in an effort to lose weight but had not successfully solved her problem. Then, as she learned how to trust and take care of herself, she began to heal herself by expressing her suppressed feelings. At a weekly support group that I led, she was encouraged to express herself directly, saying what she felt and what she wanted. She began to trust her body and started eating only what she really wanted. She grew physically and spiritually lighter, and after a few months, she had lost about forty pounds.

At this point, she thought she'd gotten all she needed from the group and wanted to drop out, even though she was still carrying a lot of excess weight. I felt that she was still holding back a lot of feelings, however, so I encouraged her to express what she was still "waiting" to say. She shared that three members in the group had started to bother her and she didn't feel safe in sharing her feelings with them. They reminded her of people and painful events from her past. In them, she saw her husband, her son, and herself mirrored. They reminded her of things she had not said or done. They reminded her of self-betrayal. Because of this, she felt angry every time she looked at them.

I encouraged her to work with me privately on these issues, and if she was willing, to come back to the group and express her feelings with group members. She needed to say what she had not said in the past. She did do this. Because of this, she began to heal her old emotional wounds and forgive herself for the past. Her energy is no longer tied to the past, so it can move more freely through her body. She continued to lose weight without overly restrictive dieting.

PACING WITH FOOD

People use food to pace their natural energy level. If you're a person who has too much nervous energy, you may use it to slow yourself down, or if you feel a need for a pick-me-up, you may use it for that. Both ultimately lead to a partial suppression of your true energy.

People are generally frightened of their power and energy, so they feel the need to pace the degree to which it flows through them. Some people use food to do this. Others use drugs, alcohol, relationships, work, or various other addictions. As people become more willing to experience and express their natural energy, the need to use food or other substances in this way will lessen.

APPRECIATING YOUR BODY

Appreciate the beauty in your body and in yourself, today. Focus on what you do like about yourself. The more willing you are to do this, the easier it will become. Your body will respond to this appreciation and grow increasingly beautiful.

It's become a habit to see what needs to be changed about ourselves. We're waiting for perfection before we'll love ourselves completely. You can change these self-critical tapes by looking at what you like about yourself and giving yourself positive feedback.

If you have trouble appreciating yourself, start by looking at others who have the same qualities you have and admire them.

A friend of mine who considered herself twenty pounds overweight was continually putting herself down for the way she looked. She felt the only way she could possibly like herself would be if she were thin. Because she could not see her own beauty, she thought she'd start by looking at women who had a similar body type and learn to appreciate them. She started to see how beautiful other "overweight" women were and noticed how sensual and alive they looked. She started complimenting others on their looks. By doing this, she could look at her own body in a new way. She began to accept and appreciate herself. Her body responded to this approval with more life and energy. She gradually lost a few pounds and has continued to appreciate her body as it is.

RITUAL FOR LOVING YOUR BODY

Stand naked in front of a full-length mirror. Send positive thoughts to every part of your body. Even if you don't like your body, or don't approve of certain parts of your body, look for something of beauty in every part of yourself. Realize that your body has been serving you for years. Thank your body for its service.

For example, you might say to yourself, "You have beautiful, thick, shiny hair." Then look in the mirror at your hair and see its beauty, its shine and glow — even if it isn't shining and glowing as much as you'd like. Continue to appreciate yourself as you are, saying, "I love the way you look. You have beautiful hands. You have strong healthy legs. You have clear skin. You have shining eyes."

Run through each part of your body in this way and really send it love and appreciation. Find a way to appreciate every part of yourself. And thank your body for being with you for however many years, following your desires and serving you. It has been doing for you what you have asked of it. If you like, you can play music that you love and use candles or flowers while performing this ritual. Do this ritual once or twice a day for at least a week. This ritual shows your body how much you appreciate and respect it. Your body has been criticized, judged, and rejected by you for years. It will respond quickly to love and energy. You will feel lighter and more energized. You will start looking more beautiful. The lines in your face will relax. You will start to glow with strength and health. You will be amazed at the results of loving your body.

Exercise

1. List all the ways you see yourself waiting (weighting). What are you waiting to say, do, have, or become?

2. Next to each item on your list, write how you can take action. What can you do to change the waiting into saying, doing, or having what you want now?

Chapter Twenty

TRANSFORMING OUR WORLD

*T*ransformation begins on an individual level and moves out into the world. The more I'm learning to trust my intuition and act on it, and the more I'm willing to experience and accept all my feelings, the more the energy of the universe can move through me. As it comes through, it heals and transforms me and everyone and everything around me.

This is true for each one of us. The more you are willing to trust and be yourself, the more life energy will move through you. Everyone around you will benefit from your energy and begin to trust and be more themselves. In turn, they become powerful channels for everyone in their sphere of influence. And so, transformation spreads rapidly throughout the world.

You may have heard of the "hundredth-monkey phenomenon." Although certain facts of this story are debated, I believe it is a powerful example of evolution and what is possible as we continue to focus on expanding our consciousness.

In Japan in 1952, scientists were studying the behavior of wild monkeys. The principal food of these monkeys was sweet potatoes. One day, they noticed one monkey do something they had never seen before — she washed her potato before she ate it. She repeated this behavior on subsequent days, and soon they noticed several other monkeys washing their potatoes before eating them. More and more monkeys began to do this. Then in 1958, after all monkeys on the island were exhibiting this new behavior, scientists on nearby islands began to report that monkeys on their islands were also beginning to wash their potatoes. There was no physical connection between the islands, and no one had transported any monkeys from one island to another.

This study illustrates something of overwhelmingly powerful importance for the human race and for our planet. Washing potatoes was a new level of evolution for these monkeys, and when enough of them had accepted it, it was apparently transferred to the monkeys on surrounding islands without any physical contact or direct communication.

This is how the evolution of consciousness takes place. Every individual's consciousness is connected to, and is a part of, the mass consciousness. When a small but significant number of individuals have moved into a new level of awareness and significantly changed their behavior, that change is felt in the entire mass consciousness. Every other individual is then moved in the direction of that change. And the whole thing may have started with one individual who first made the leap.

So often we look at the world around us and feel terribly helpless to effect any significant positive change. The world seems so big, and in such a mess, and we feel so small and powerless. The hundredth-monkey story helps us to see how powerful one individual, or a few individuals, can be in transforming the world.

Because the world truly is our mirror, as we change, it must change. You can see this easily in your personal life. As you develop the habit of trusting and taking care of yourself, you will gradually release your old patterns. Soon you notice that your friends, family, and business associates all seem to be feeling and acting differently, as well. Things that previously frightened and upset you seem to have lost their emotional "charge." Even the serious problems of the world, while they still concern you, may not seem quite as scary as before.

The reason for this shift is that you are beginning to feel the power of the universe inside of you. To the degree that you experience the presence of the universe in your own body, you don't feel afraid. Of course, every time you open up to more power, more of the old fear gets flushed to the surface and released, so in the healing process, you will experience alternating states of power and fear. Gradually, however, a solid base of trust will be established within you. Others will feel this and in it will find the support to open up to more of their own power and truth. The people and things around you will reflect you in increasingly positive ways. The more light you allow within you, the brighter the world you live in will be.

CREATING THE CHANGE

One idea I frequently encounter, especially in groups of spiritually oriented people, is that all we have to do to change
the world is think more positively about it and visualize the
change we desire. Visualization and affirmation are powerful tools. I use them often and strongly recommend them as
part of this process. (After all, I wrote *Creative Visualization*
and I deeply believe in the effectiveness of the techniques it
describes.) There is another part of the process that is frequently ignored, however, yet it is just as important.

If the world is our mirror, then whatever we see out there
in some way reflects what is in us. We must take responsibility
for it and be willing to transform it *within ourselves* if we want
to see it change on the outside. So when we look at the world
and see poverty, pain, violence, and chaos, we must be willing
to say to ourselves, "What is the poverty, pain, violence, and
chaos within me that this is reflecting? I know that my world
is my mirror and, in a sense, my creation. If the things I see
weren't in me, they couldn't exist in the world."

The trick here is not to take on *blame* or *guilt* for the
world's problems. None of us is truly responsible for other
people's lives; we are all co-creating this world together. And
we are all doing the best we know how. We are here to learn
from what is not perfect rather than blame ourselves for it. We
need to adopt a positive attitude of responsibility, saying, "I
am willing to learn to trust and follow my own inner truth,
knowing that as I do, I will release the pain and fear within me
and thus heal the pain and fear in the world."

Such a vow is very powerful, and to follow through on it

is no easy task. To do so, we must be willing to move through the deepest layers of our consciousness and recognize not only our own personal fears but also centuries-old negative beliefs of humanity that exist in our bodies. To move through these layers, we need to be willing to recognize and experience all the fears, knowing that the light is healing and dissolving them.

When people ask me what they can do about the problems of the world, I suggest that they start by recognizing and affirming that as they sincerely do their own inner work, the world is being transformed. I tell them to look at the social problems that frighten or disturb them and determine what fear or pain it touches within them and how it reflects their personal situation.

For example, if they are disturbed by reports of violence, I ask them to look at how violence has played a part in their lives. Has someone been violent toward them in their early years? Have they had violent thoughts and feelings? Have they repressed or disassociated from their own violent feelings? In what way have they done violence to themselves internally (harshly criticizing themselves, and so on)?

It has been my experience that many of us need help, in the form of supportive therapy or counseling, to deal with deep levels of emotional healing. For some people, there's a certain reluctance to seek such help, perhaps because they fear it's an indication of sickness or craziness. Our culture tells us that we should be totally self-sufficient and that needing help is a sign of weakness. In reality, we all need support at times, and it is a sign of strength to reach out for appropriate help. Personally, I have sought therapy of various types at many times in my life and it has helped me greatly, as long as I trusted my own intuition about who to work with.

If you are deeply touched by the poverty in which much of the world's population is currently living, you may feel moved to make some external gestures to help alleviate someone's pain (i.e., contribute some money, do some social or political work). At the same time, look within yourself to see in what way you believe in, or support, poverty or scarcity in your own life. This may not be a question of money — you may be living in some form of emotional or spiritual poverty while surrounded by material luxury. Or you may be at peace spiritually and emotionally but holding on to a belief that money is evil, thus keeping yourself in a state of financial poverty.

Poverty, on both a personal and worldwide level, is supported by our mass consciousness belief in scarcity. We deeply fear that there is *not enough to go around* of whatever we need — money, food, love, energy, appreciation. So we create a world that supports that belief. There have been studies that show that there is plenty of food produced in this world to amply feed everyone. Yet, because of our underlying belief in poverty, we allow food to be thrown away in one place while millions are starving to death elsewhere.

If you are concerned by environmental issues, consider this point of view: Mother Nature is symbolic of the nurturing, feminine aspect of ourselves. Disrespect and lack of harmony with nature are only possible in a society of individuals who disrespect and disregard their own feminine, intuitive nature. If you are attuned to your inner guidance, there is no way you can become severely out of balance with your natural environment.

Just as our bodies are the manifestation of our consciousness in physical form, the earth is the manifestation of our
mass consciousness. In a sense, the earth is our collective
"body." The way we treat her mirrors the way we treat our
own bodies.

The lack of respect and attunement afforded to our bodies is demonstrated on a global level by the way we treat our
earth. Until we learn to love and trust our bodies, to listen to
their signals, to give them the food, rest, and nurturing they
need, to stop polluting them with drugs and unwholesome
food, and to stop trying to control them with our ideas about
what's right, I believe we will continue to mistreat our "earth
body."

We must be willing to recognize and heal any form of violence, poverty, and imbalance within ourselves as individuals
if we hope to eradicate these problems from our world. Healing does not take place on a personal or planetary level as
long as we hide or deny our feelings. All feelings, beliefs, and
emotional patterns must be brought to the light of consciousness in order to be transformed. When the light shines into the
darkness, the darkness disappears.

WORLD HEALING

People frequently talk about what terrible shape the world is
in. In many ways, things seem to be going from bad to worse,
and this can be very frightening. It has helped me consider-
ably to recognize that the world is currently going through a

major healing crisis, very similar in form to what many individuals are experiencing.

When we as individuals begin to wake up to the light, we also begin to become aware of the darkness in which we have been living. The patterns of living that formerly seemed "normal" begin to look crazier and crazier from the perspective of our newly acquired sanity. Fears and distortions that have been denied and ignored because they were too painful to look at begin to come into our consciousness in order to be released. Problems that were swept under the rug come forth to be solved.

This is what I see happening on a worldwide level today. If we recognize the seeming chaos and pain in the world as a giant manifestation of our individual healing process, we can see that it's a very positive step. Rather than feeling like victims, we can recognize the power of the universe at work. We can appreciate ourselves as channels through which the world's healing is being manifested.*

SOCIAL AND POLITICAL ACTION

Some who have heard these ideas become angry because they believe I am endorsing a narcissistic self-absorption that denies the problems of the world and negates the necessity of social and political action. Upon further discussion, I am usually (though not always!) able to make them understand that

---

* For more of my thoughts on this topic, read *The Path of Transformation: How Healing Ourselves Can Change the World.*

this is not the case. Being willing to deal internally and individually with the original source of the problem is simply the most practical and powerful way to effect real change. It does not deny the necessity of external action on a large scale.

The issue for me is the source and motivation for that action. I find that people are frequently moved by their own "good ideas" more than by their inner guidance. Often they are motivated by their feelings of pain, fear, and guilt into wanting to do something to make it better. They are coming from a position of helplessness and fear, struggling vainly to do something to eradicate these feelings. Unfortunately, this approach only perpetuates the problem it is trying to solve.

The underlying cause of the world problems is the pain, fear, and ignorance we experience from being disconnected from the power of the universe. If we continue to project our problems outside of ourselves and fail to recognize the inner power we actually have, I believe we will support the very evils we are fighting.

On the other hand, if we are willing to take responsibility for our fears and deal with them, we will clear the way for being able to hear the voice of the universe within us. If it tells us to take action, we can be sure the action will be powerful and truly effective.

For example, a woman friend of mine became very active in the nuclear disarmament movement. When she talked about the issue and her work, it was obvious that she was feeling absolutely terrified of the possibility of nuclear war. This is actually a reasonable reaction, given the world situation. The problem, as I saw it, was that she was not recognizing her own terror and the issues of powerlessness and death that she was struggling with internally. So her actions and words had a frantic quality — almost like a drowning person's clutching vainly for something to hold on to.

Gradually, over several years, I saw her work through this phase of her process. I believe that she reached a deeper level of trust in the universe. She continued her anti-nuclear activity because it was something she deeply believed in, and found great satisfaction in doing so, but the energy was quite different. There was power and strength in her involvement, which I'm certain made her more effective in her work.

The same principles hold true in the social and political arena as in every other area of life: If you are doing what you think you should do, if you are motivated primarily by fear and guilt, then no matter how good your actions, you are probably not being as effective as you'd like to be, and you may even be hindering more than you are helping.

On the other hand, if you are trusting your intuition and following your heart — going where your energy takes you and doing what you really want to do — you will see that *everything* you do has a positive effect in changing the world. You will be able to recognize the transformational nature of your actions. For many, this will include direct social and political action, and you'll be doing it because you love it! People around you will also be affected by your energy and vitality even more than they are affected by your words and actions.

For now, my inner guidance has told me that living my life as I do — writing books, leading workshops, exploring my creativity, being myself — is what I personally need to be doing to effect maximum change in my life and the world. I've also gotten a strong feeling that I may someday be actively involved in politics (as I was earlier in my life) — perhaps even occupy a political office of some sort! Although I have no particular desire to do this at this time, I know that if that's what I'm meant to do, I'll find it an exciting adventure. I'm curious to see what the universe has in store for me.

A FIVE-STEP PROCESS FOR PERSONAL AND PLANETARY HEALING

1. Affirm to yourself: *The power of the universe is healing and transforming me. As I am healed and transformed, the whole world is healed and transformed.*

2. Notice the social, political, and environmental issues around you. Pay particular attention to those that trigger the most emotional reaction in you. Ask to see how they may reflect your personal issues, fears, beliefs, and patterns. You may not immediately see any connection, but stay open to receiving this information through your intuitive channel.

3. Ask for the higher power of the universe to release and heal the ignorance, fear, and limitation within you and in the world. Be open to any inner guidance you may receive to seek support in your healing process through a counselor or therapist, friends, a workshop or group, or in any other form.

4. Regularly visualize your life and the world as you would like them to be (see the meditation at the end of this chapter).

5. Ask your inner guidance to let you know clearly if there is any specific action you need to take toward your own, or the world's, healing. Then continue to trust and follow your intuition, knowing that you will be led to do whatever is necessary.

Meditation

Sit or lie in a comfortable position. Take a few deep breaths and relax your body. Feel yourself dropping into a deep, quiet place within. Feel yourself contacting that place of power and creativity, your source of strength.

From this source of strength, project yourself into the future, a few years or more, and in this projection, imagine your life exactly the way you want it to be.

Start by noticing how you feel spiritually and emotionally. Feel the strength and power within you. You trust your intuition and act on your inner guidance. Because of this, your life is unfolding in a wonderful way.

Get a sense of your body. How do you look and feel physically? You now have a body that matches your spirit — strong, courageous, beautiful, filled with life and energy. Experience what that feels like. How do you take care of your body? What do you eat and how do you nurture yourself?

Imagine yourself dressed exactly the way you want to be dressed. Your clothes express who you are. When you open your closets and drawers, you have just the clothes you want there.

What is your home like? See yourself living exactly where you want to be. You have created your environment as you want it. Feel what it's like to live in a way that suits you perfectly.

You have found the perfect job and creative outlet. Imagine expressing yourself in a way that brings you fulfillment and satisfaction. You receive an abundance of money for doing what you most love.

You now have relationships that are honest, alive, passionate, and creative. People love and nurture you. If you have (or want to have) a special partner in your life, imagine that relationship as you would like it to be.

Now remember that the world is your mirror. As you are growing and changing, so is the world around you. In fact, you are part of the mass consciousness that is creating the world. So let yourself imagine the world healing and transforming, coming into balance, wholeness, and harmony, just as you are.

Chapter Twenty-One

MY VISION

*M*y vision, is that as we continue to do our own work, we build a future together that overflows with possibility. That through integrating all of who we are, we can experience abundance, fulfillment, and limitless resources to heal and create the new world. The momentum of this growth pushes aside old structures, belief systems, and ideas to make way for the expansive horizon now emerging. We are guided by the light.

Acknowledgments

My heartfelt appreciation goes to Gina Vucci for her creative ideas, moral support, and hard work in helping me shape the 25th anniversary edition of *Living in the Light*.

Thanks also to my editor, Georgia Hughes; my publisher, Marc Allen; and all the other supportive people at New World Library.

Most of all, I thank my readers. Over the years, your feedback about how this book has affected your lives has been my inspiration and my reward.

Recommended Resources

BOOKS

Gawain, Shakti. *Creating True Prosperity*. Nataraj/New World Library, 1997.

———. *Creative Visualization*, 25th anniversary edition. Nataraj/New World Library, 2002.

———. *The Four Levels of Healing: A Guide to Balancing the Spiritual, Mental, Emotional, and Physical Aspects of Life*. Nataraj/New World Library, 1997.

———. *The Path of Transformation: How Healing Ourselves Can Change the World*, revised edition. Nataraj/New World Library, 1993, 2000.

Roberts, Jane. *The Nature of Personal Reality*. Amber-Allen Publishing/New World Library, 1994.

Stone, Hal, and Sidra Stone. *Embracing Each Other: Relationship as Teacher, Healer, and Guide*. Nataraj/New World Library, 1993.
———. *Embracing Our Selves: The Voice Dialogue Manual*. Nataraj/New World Library, 1993.
Stone, Sidra. *The Shadow King*. Nataraj/New World Library, 1997.

AUDIOS

Gawain, Shakti. *Creative Visualization*. Nataraj/New World Library, 1995.
———. *Creative Visualization Meditations*. Nataraj/New World Library, 1996.
———. *Living in the Light*. Nataraj/New World Library, 1998.
———. *Meditations for Creating True Prosperity*. Nataraj/New World Library, 1997.
Stone, Hal, and Sidra Stone. *Affairs and Attractions*. Delos, 1990.
———. *The Child Within*. Delos, 1990.
———. *The Dance of Selves in Relationship*. Delos, 1990.
———. *Meeting Your Selves*. Delos, 1990.
———. *Meet the Pusher*. Delos, 1990.
———. *Meet Your Inner Critic*. Delos, 1990.
———. *Understanding Your Relationships*. Delos, 1990.

(Shakti Gawain's audios are available through ShaktiGawain.com, NewWorldLibrary.com, and/or Audible.com. All of Hal and Sidra Stone's audios are available through Delos. See contact information on next page.)

WORKSHOPS

Shakti Gawain gives talks and leads workshops all over the United States and in many other countries. She also conducts retreats, intensives, and training programs. If you would like to be on her mailing list and receive workshop information, contact:

Shakti Gawain, Inc.
PO Box 377, Mill Valley, CA 94942
Telephone: (415) 888-8320
staff@shaktigawain.com
www.shaktigawain.com

For information about Drs. Hal and Sidra Stone's workshops and trainings, contact:

Delos
PO Box 604, Albion, CA 95410
Telephone: (707) 937-2424
info@voicedialogue.org
www.delos-inc.com

About the Author

*S*hakti Gawain is a pioneer in the field of personal development. For over thirty years, she has been a bestselling author and an internationally renowned teacher of consciousness. Shakti has worked with thousands of individuals in developing greater awareness, balance, and wholeness in their lives.

Shakti has written numerous books that are considered classics. Her distinguished publishing history includes the bestsellers *Creative Visualization*, *The Path of Transformation*, *Four Levels of Healing*, *Creating True Prosperity*, and *Developing Intuition*. Her books have sold over ten million copies and have been translated into more than thirty languages. She is the cofounder, with Marc Allen, of New World Library, a publishing company based in Northern California.

She has appeared on such nationally syndicated programs as *The Oprah Winfrey Show*, *Good Morning America*, *Sonya Live*, *The Larry King Show*, *The Leeza Show*, *America's Talking*, and New Dimensions Radio and has been featured in *New Woman*, *New Age Journal*, and *Time* magazine.

Through her seminars and her books, Shakti helps people heal and develop all levels of their being — spiritual, mental, emotional, physical — and access their intuitive inner wisdom. Sharing the ideas and practices that have helped her the most in her own life, she guides others on their path to living more consciously. She facilitates their process of finding deeper meaning and purpose through developing their unique gifts and abilities.

Shakti is a passionate environmentalist who believes that as we bring more awareness to our daily lives, we can learn to live in balance with our planet. She and her husband, Jim Burns, live in Mill Valley, California.

NEW WORLD LIBRARY is dedicated to publishing books and other media that inspire and challenge us to improve the quality of our lives and the world.

We are a socially and environmentally aware company, and we strive to embody the ideals presented in our publications. We recognize that we have an ethical responsibility to our customers, our staff members, and our planet.

We serve our customers by creating the finest publications possible on personal growth, creativity, spirituality, wellness, and other areas of emerging importance. We serve New World Library employees with generous benefits, significant profit sharing, and constant encouragement to pursue their most expansive dreams.

As a member of the Green Press Initiative, we print an increasing number of books with soy-based ink on 100 percent postconsumer-waste recycled paper. Also, we power our offices with solar energy and contribute to nonprofit organizations working to make the world a better place for us all.

Our products are available
in bookstores everywhere.
For our catalog, please contact:

New World Library
14 Pamaron Way
Novato, California 94949

Phone: 415-884-2100 or 800-972-6657
Catalog requests: Ext. 50
Orders: Ext. 52
Fax: 415-884-2199
Email: escort@newworldlibrary.com

To subscribe to our electronic newsletter, visit
www.newworldlibrary.com